*Marie Simms Lee*

# HOME IN GOD'S COUNTRY

A Novel
Not a Memoir

Marie Lee

Copyright © 2021 by Marie Lee

All rights reserved.

In Loving Memory

Of

Donald and Darlene Simms

# TABLE OF CONTENTS

Acknowledgement..................................................1
Prologue......................................................3
1. A Country Girl's First Day of First Grade ................5
2. Discoveries ............................................13
3. A New Decade ..........................................21
4. An Angel at the South School ..........................31
5. Waiting for Raymond George ............................39
6. Remembering Grandpa Brown .............................47
7. The Red Dress .........................................55
8. Visitors From the East ................................63
9. Winter Sets In ........................................71
10. What She Learned .....................................79
11. A New Normal .........................................87
12. Lessons of Spring ....................................95
13. One Season at a Time ................................103
14. Last Shuffle to the South School ....................111
15. Mountains to Climb, Rivers to Cross .................121
16. Mamma Comes Home ....................................131
17. Blackie and Silver ..................................139
18. Sonny ...............................................149
19. The River of Life ...................................159
20. Growing Up Close to Heaven ..........................167
21. The Grand Tour ......................................177
22. At Home in God's Country ............................187
23. Endings and Beginnings ..............................197

# ACKNOWLEDGEMENT

Thank you to the descendants of Bernice Gunther Wallace Osburn for the use of her painting as a cover for this book. Bernice was Donald's cousin and she loved the ranch beneath the rim. Her painting is a perfect depiction of how the barnyard looked during the 1950s.

# PROLOGUE

Branding—2021

"We're gonna put the cows thru there, Aunt Marie."

"Ok. I'll hold the gate."

"Aunt Marie," Dustin, more patient than he has probably been with anyone in a long time, drily and gently explained, "they won't go thru with you standin' there."

It's official! I have become a city slicker, more ignorant in the ways of a cow than any country girl should ever become.

I moved on down the fence to a more distant location and watched, mesmerized by the intricate dance and team work of horses and riders as they cut out the cows, pushed them through the gate and worked calves back to the interior of the corral. My next problem: I couldn't figure out how to work that blasted Powder River gate to get inside the corral, but about that same time along came a young couple with horses in tow who flipped the gate open and I slid through with them. I finally made it to branding headquarters with no further incidents.

It's been a long time since I attended a branding at the SC Ranch. It was about like I remembered.

The sky was crystal blue, probably more so than it ought to be because if it doesn't rain soon, we are in for some deep trouble this summer. There was a bite to April's north wind, but in the shelter of the horse trailer and pickup it wasn't half-bad. There was a good mixture of cowboys and cowgirls who are handy with a rope, ear-tags, vaccine guns and a sharp knife. The horses looked good, acted good and knew what they were supposed to do.

The whole thing went like clock-work from my point of view.

There's a newer, more efficient kind of branding fire since the last time I was in a branding corral. The fire was in a long metal stove, off the ground, and four branding irons roasted in the coals. Off to the side was a cooler filled with water bottles and Gator Ade and another cooler held a more adult type of thirst quencher. On the prep table rested a mixture of vaccines for various diseases and ear tags along with other assorted branding paraphernalia plus plastic containers of homemade cookies to tide everyone over 'til dinner-time.

There was no lag time in this operation.

There were consistently two calves stretched between horses and ropers. A team moved swiftly from one calf to the next as they vaccinated, marked for vaccination with a streak of fluorescent pink chalk, ear-marked, ear-tagged and altered bull calves into steers.

I noticed something. Something that brought a tiny spark of pride to my old sentimental soul while I watched my brother, Sonny, do his work on the ground as he, and he alone, placed the Lazy SC on the right hip of each calf. I thought back to the days when it was Dad who applied the branding iron to SC Ranch calves.

In another observation I noticed that it was my nephew who actually ramrodded the whole affair. He and his wife being the next generation at the ranch. Caitlin, my niece-in-law, wielded vaccine guns and had dinner under control up at the house.

For an old has-been ranch girl who doesn't know how to operate a gate or stay clear of cows nowadays, I had more fun on Friday morning than I can explain. Dust and dried cow manure caked my shoes and my jeans. My cell-phone camera was caked with dust, my face and my hair were filled with dust, I smelled like a branding fire and clear through the next day everything tasted a little bit like scorched hair. I'm downright sorry for those who don't understand, because life doesn't get much better.

# Home In God's Country

## A Country Girl's First Day of First Grade

She was scared and excited all at the same time. For months Mommy had been telling her, and Grandmo had too, about how much she was going to like school, but still, she did not know what to expect. Kids who lived in town went to kindergarten but very few country kids began their education at that level, and now here it was—the first day of first grade.

She had no older brothers or sisters to pave the way and her only frame of reference came from Mommy and Daddy and Grandmo and Grandpo. She knew Mike Counts and Madge Schofield. They lived down near the store. It was their first day too, but Mike had his older brother, John, and Madge had older brothers and sisters. Madge and Mike were nervous also.

She wanted to learn how to read and write. She had a vague notion about math and geography and she had been told that there were lots and lots of other things that she would learn someday. She figured that when the right time came along, she would know. For today, reading and writing were the most important.

Marie's mother was Darlene Simms and when Marie was a little girl, she called her mother "Mommy."

Mommy told Marie that even though the school knew she was coming she would have to go to school with her on the first day so that she could officially enroll her. Darlene knew how to drive and she could do so in a pinch, but for a vague reason that seemed to include a wreck in her early driving career with a teenage boyfriend's car, she preferred not to and did not have a driver's license. Because of all that, Daddy, whose name was Donald Simms, left off harvesting grain that morning so that he could drive Mommy into town.

It was four miles from the ranch down to the Valley Falls Store where Vest Carroll, who drove the school bus, began the Valley Falls route. Donald pulled the car up beside the store and Marie jumped out to join Madge and Mike who were already in line to board the bus.

Donald and Darlene watched until Marie was safely on the bus and then Donald whipped the car on around the bus and headed toward town.

She was almost as excited about riding the bus as she was about going to school. As far as she was concerned, riding that little pint-sized bright yellow school bus was a major part of the whole package.

In those days there was still a Valley Falls School District Number Nine and the district owned the bus. It was a stubby little bus, almost comical appearing when driven up beside the school buses owned by Lake County School District Number Seven. Some laughed and called it "pint-sized." When the pint-sized bus pulled up in front of the school everyone knew that the Valley Falls kids had arrived.

Vest Carroll and his wife, Bessie, owned the Valley Falls Store. Folks in the valley called it "the Store." It was a combination gas station, post office and grocery store as well as the main hub of information. With Vest driving the school bus into town he kept everyone up on Lakeview news also. Whenever Donald or his father, whose name was Lytle Simms, picked up the mail they usually took time for a cold beer, or a soda, so that they could catch up on the latest. They leaned with their elbows propped on Bessie's glass counters as they picked up tidbits of information.

It's at the Valley Falls Store where Oregon State Highway 31 junctions off and heads north, straight as an arrow, while Highway 395 veers off to the right and heads toward Abert Lake and out across the desert to Burns. The Schofield family lived across the junction from the store and the Counts family lived down the county road about a quarter mile past the Schofield's.

That first morning Mrs. Schofield drove Madge across to the store and Minnie Counts walked up the road with John and Mike. Minnie was scheduled to ride into town with Mrs. Schofield so that they could register Madge and Mike in school.

For folks who lived out in Valley Falls there never was a hard and fast rule of etiquette when it came to the proper usage of names and titles. With that being the case, it was never understood but simply the way it was that Mrs. Schofield, whose name was Florence, was always called "Mrs. Schofield," while Mr. Schofield, whose name was Jake, was called "Jake." Minnie Counts, on the other hand, was "Minnie," to one and all and it followed that her husband, Gay, was also called by his first name. Donald and Darlene Simms, who were somewhat younger, were always known by their first names. Marie's grandparents were Lottie and Lytle. A few, but not many, called Lottie, Mrs. Simms, while Lytle was Lytle to one and all except to Marie who called them "Grandpo and Grandmo."

Madge and Marie sat together in the seat behind Vest while Mike sat with John across the aisle. The little girls held hands as they carefully looked over each student who boarded the bus. There were other little girls and little boys just like them, who were nervous and scared, but most were older and confident of their rightful place in the hierarchy of Valley Falls bus students. The high school boys swaggered down the aisle and plopped in the seat of their personal choice. When Vest pulled up to the North School the bus was filled to capacity and a voice could scarcely be heard above the clamor and din.

It's twenty-three miles from Valley Falls to Lakeview.

In 1949 there were two elementary schools in Lakeview—the North School and the South School. Valley Falls elementary students went to the North School because they arrived from the north and children who lived south of the division line which was, as far as I can remember, Center Street, were enrolled in the South School.

When she stepped off the bus Mommy was there to take Marie's hand and they proceeded to the principal's office for registration.

The principal was Mrs. Laura Barry. To Marie, Mrs. Barry appeared tall and on the verge of outlandish. Her bright colored dresses rustled and swished as she walked. Her high-heeled shoes clicked and clacked as she hurried through hallways over shiny polished floors. Bracelets jingled and jangled, necklaces of bright colored beads and golden chains hung from her neck while her earrings dangled and bobbed as they caught the occasional glint of light. Her black hair was streaked, here and there, with grey. She wore bright red lipstick and there was a definite spot of pink rouge on each cheek. Laura Barry made an impact—there was no doubt about that. She was a strict disciplinarian, but on the other hand she was jolly and her laughter rang through the halls. It turned out that even the most-timid among first-grade students was soon happy to be at her school.

Mrs. Barry's voice was loud, somewhat like old Bill Kimzey, Marie thought, who was hard of hearing and so he yelled at everyone else. And the sound of her voice was a bit raspy. Madge, Mike and Marie gulped as she leaned down to shake hands with them. She called them each by name, however, and bid them welcome to the North School.

Even though Marie did not know Mrs. Barry, Mrs. Barry seemed to know who she was. That night when Marie told Grandmo about Mrs. Barry Grandmo said that she'd known Laura Barry for years and years and that she was a good teacher.

"Mrs. Simms," Mrs. Barry said to Mommy, "I am happy to have Marie in our school. Although she will be in Mrs. Zevely's classroom I am so delighted to see her. Mrs. Zevely is a fine teacher and you will like her immediately. By the way, how are Lottie and Lytle? I haven't seen them for ages. Please give them my best."

She said all of this in one great rush. Marie looked up at her mother and Mommy smiled a soft reassuring smile down to her anxious daughter.

"Mom and Dad are fine and they are excited, along with Donald and me, to have Marie going to school."

Mommy laid her hand on Marie's shoulder and said, "Be a good girl now, and have a wonderful day. Either Daddy, or Grandpo, or Grandmo will be waiting for you at the store this evening."

Mrs. Schofield and Minnie left too and Marie, Madge and Mike were left with Mrs. Barry to guide their next steps. She motioned for them to follow as she click-clacked down the hallway. They went down the stairs and found out that the lunch room was to the left but they turned right where Mrs. Barry opened the door to Mrs. Zevely's room.

Mrs. Zevely's room was in the basement. Later Marie learned that it was an overflow classroom put in at the last minute because there were so many incoming first-grade students. Lakeview's school system was overflowing with school-aged children born during the war.

There were windows that let in streams of morning sun but they were odd because they were level with the sidewalk outside. Mrs. Zevely had decorated her room with plants and bright, happy pictures and posters with big and small ABC's and numbers. It was the happiest room that Marie had ever encountered.

"Mrs. Zevely," Mrs. Barry said in her booming voice, "this is Mike Counts, Madge Schofield and Marie Simms. They will be in your room this year," and with that she turned and click-clacked back up the stairs.

Mrs. Zevely was the exact opposite of Mrs. Barry. In fact, Marie thought that Mrs. Zevely was somewhat like Grandmo. She was small, neat and her soft hair waved back to a bun at the base of her neck. She smiled over the rim of her glasses at her new students and said in a firm, sweet voice, "Welcome to my classroom. I am so glad to see you. You may place your things at your desk and your lunchboxes on the bench by the door and then you may run outside and play with the others until the school bell rings."

All in that instant Marie knew that she was going to love Mrs. Zevely.

Madge and Marie marveled at all the wonderful fun things in the playground. Madge knew about playgrounds but Marie did not know until that day that there would be a slide, a merry-go-round, a teeter-totter, a set of monkey bars and great swings on long chains. The swings that she knew about were a tire-swing hung in Grandmo's big maple tree and a board slat hung with rope from a limb in front of the washhouse.

Right away she liked everything but the monkey bars—she was not bold enough to swing hand over hand from one bar to the next.

They squealed as they slid down the slick metal slide. They hit the ground with a thump and even though it was great fun both Madge and Marie suddenly discovered that they had smudged the edges of their new school dresses. They had been cautioned, perhaps cautioned a little too much, that they had to take care of their new dresses. They had been told over and over that little girls were expected to stay clean and neat—they should not be seen with smudges on their knees, or their hands and certainly not on their dresses.

They looked at each other with panic but Madge said, "I know where the bathroom is. Hurry, we can wash before the bell rings."

They rushed inside to the girls' restroom and tore off paper towels in a desperate attempt to remove the tell-tale smudges from the edges of their dresses and clean up their hands and knees. How could they have been so careless to get dirty before school even began?! And then the bell rang. Marie felt like crying and staying in the bathroom but Madge was the braver of the two and she encouraged, "Don't worry. I'm sure we're clean enough."

She was somewhat bolstered up when it turned out that no one, not even Mrs. Zevely, noticed that her dress had a trace of school yard dirt on the edge of the hem.

Their newly established basement classroom had been outfitted with the latest style of modern desks designed especially for small children. She had never imagined a desk as wonderful as those, in fact, they were not a desk at all. They were tables that came apart in sections and then rejoined to form circles, oblongs and squares. The wood was light blond and there was a little chair for each student. There were cubby holes built under the tables—one for each student to place books, rulers, tablets and pencils.

Marie's seat was at a round table with two boys and another little girl and by the first recess they knew each other's names.

That first day flew by but it was also very long.

Mrs. Zevely was aware that neither Marie nor Mike had attended kindergarten. Madge, whose older married sister lived in town, had attended most of her kindergarten year. Right away Mrs. Zevely began to tutor Mike and Marie after school while they waited for the school bus to arrive with the older junior-high and high-school students.

She was tired when the bus drove up to the store that evening and Marie was glad that it was Grandpo who was waiting there to pick her up. He was her hero.

When Marie was a child Lytle Simms appeared to her as Prince Charming did to Cinderella. She listened to a record about Cinderella on Grandmo's and Grandpo's fancy new record player hour after hour. She didn't understand it, of course, that that's how she felt about her grandfather—she simply worshiped the ground on which he walked. Many, many years later Marie figured out that Lytle Simms was all of that and even more to her grandmother. He was tall, straight and possessed of a full head of wavy black hair that was now streaked with random strands of gray. His kind eyes sparked with a confidence gentled by life, wisdom and age.

Marie ran to him and he bent down to gather her close. She threw her arms around his neck relieved, at long last, for the security of home.

"How was school?"

"It was wonderful, Grandpo. I learned a lot today! You should see the swings and the merry-go-round. The desks are little tables and chairs, and I learned how the letter 'A' sounds and clear down the alphabet to the letter 'E.' My teacher's name is Mrs. Zevely and she's a real nice lady. I'm really hungry, Grandpo! Can I get something to eat?"

It all whooshed out in one breath and then she took a big gulp of air. Lytle laughed at her excitement. "Run in the store an' you can get a package of cupcakes while I pick up the mail."

and then rejoined to form circles, oblongs and squares. The wood was light blond and there was a little chair for each student. There were cubby holes built under the tables—one for each student to place books, rulers, tablets and pencils.

Marie's seat was at a round table with two boys and another little girl and by the first recess they knew each other's names.

That first day flew by but it was also very long.

Mrs. Zevely was aware that neither Marie nor Mike had attended kindergarten. Madge, whose older married sister lived in town, had attended most of her kindergarten year. Right away Mrs. Zevely began to tutor Mike and Marie after school while they waited for the school bus to arrive with the older junior-high and high-school students.

She was tired when the bus drove up to the store that evening and Marie was glad that it was Grandpo who was waiting there to pick her up. He was her hero.

When Marie was a child Lytle Simms appeared to her as Prince Charming did to Cinderella. She listened to a record about Cinderella on Grandmo's and Grandpo's fancy new record player hour after hour. She didn't understand it, of course, that that's how she felt about her grandfather—she simply worshiped the ground on which he walked. Many, many years later Marie figured out that Lytle Simms was all of that and even more to her grandmother. He was tall, straight and possessed of a full head of wavy black hair that was now streaked with random strands of gray. His kind eyes sparked with a confidence gentled by life, wisdom and age.

Marie ran to him and he bent down to gather her close. She threw her arms around his neck relieved, at long last, for the security of home.

"How was school?"

"It was wonderful, Grandpo. I learned a lot today! You should see the swings and the merry-go-round. The desks are little tables and chairs, and I learned how the letter 'A' sounds and clear down the alphabet to the letter 'E.' My teacher's name is Mrs. Zevely and she's a real nice lady. I'm really hungry, Grandpo! Can I get something to eat?"

It all whooshed out in one breath and then she took a big gulp of air. Lytle laughed at her excitement. "Run in the store an' you can get a package of cupcakes while I pick up the mail."

# Discoveries

Once the first day of first grade was over Marie gradually began to gain bits and pieces of self-confidence. She was, after all, an established member of one particular group—the bus students—she was a Valley Falls girl. In those days it was only the country kids who rode the school bus. Not long after that, when things began to change somewhat, kids out on the perimeter of town started riding the bus also. The truth of the matter was that the bus students were the fortunate ones, because town kids had to either walk or ride their bicycles no matter the weather or distance.

In Marie's opinion her first grade of school was a complete success. Very few contentions arose that year, and when she grew old and began to tell her grandchildren stories about her childhood Marie could hardly remember any troublesome thing about that entire year.

Mrs. Zevely was as kind, sweet and lovely on the last day of school as she was on the first.

She learned how to read. Not far into the year she was reading above her age-level. She learned how to print. Mrs. Zevely said that her printing was quite neat and that she constructed her sentences quite well. Arithmetic, however, was a different story. By the end of the year, she could add and subtract and most of it was correct. Mike Counts, however, excelled at arithmetic and he sailed to the head of the class. But his printing was not as neat as Marie's. Nor could he read out loud as nicely as Marie.

Mrs. Zevely asked Mrs. Scheidereiter and Mrs. Mercer to be roommothers. Mrs. Scheidereiter's son, Walt, and Mrs. Mercer's daughter, Ann, were also in Mrs. Zevely's class. They were town children and so it was more convenient for their mothers to do such things. Unlike today, in 1948 many mothers still had the ability to be stay-at-home mothers, and along with Mrs. Zevely, those room-mothers opened Marie's eyes to wonders that she had no idea existed. In particular she learned how to celebrate holidays in the most up-to-date fashion.

Marie knew about the important holidays like Thanksgiving and Christmas, but she knew little to nothing about Halloween, Valentine's Day, St. Patrick's Day, and mostly because her family were not church goers, she didn't know much about Easter either. That year Mrs. Scheidereiter, Mrs. Mercer and Mrs. Zevely educated her in ways that she never forgot.

Marie promptly carried all of her newly-found information home to Mommy, Daddy, Grandmo and Grandpo, at the ranch. They already knew about those holidays, of course, but in those days, life on a ranch or a farm, did not allow for much in the way of extra money, time or even the notion for celebrating such things as Halloween. Marie's entrance into school, however, took away their professed innocence.

Halloween was the first eye-opener. Mrs. Zevely carved a jack-o-lantern from a perfectly rounded pumpkin, brought it to school and placed it on one corner of her desk. Marie had never seen such a thing!

They learned how to trace autumn leaves on bright colored paper. Marie didn't know that the fall of year was correctly called "autumn." Everyone she knew called it "fall." "Last fall, this fall or maybe in the fall…" They made paper jack-0-lanterns, and they made masks from brown wrapping paper to wear for a thing called "trick-or-treat" that happened on Halloween night. A country girl could never go trick-or-treating, of course, but she could take those beautiful autumn leaves, paper pumpkins, and those funny masks home and show them to her family.

The best thing of all was that on Friday afternoon before Halloween Mrs. Zevely's room-mothers brought a Halloween party to school. Mrs. Scheidereiter and Mrs. Mercer were dressed in bright, funny clothes with tons and tons of flashy jewelry and wore pointy black witch hats. They served wonderful pumpkin shaped cookies with jack-o-lantern faces. They served those cookies along with candy on Halloween napkins, and poured a delicious orange colored punch into little paper cups that were decorated with ghosts, spider-webs, and witches.

It was the most wonderful afternoon of her entire life!

Marie did not ride the bus home that evening because Mommy and Grandpo and Grandmo had come to town for shopping so they stopped by the school and picked her up.

When they got home Donald helped Darlene carry in the boxes from the grocery store, and as he placed one on the kitchen table, he looked into it and said, "Darlene, what's this thing? Marie, look here!"

Daddy reached in and brought out a fat orange pumpkin!

Later, when the supper dishes were done, Mommy helped Marie cut off the top. Together they scooped out the gooey seeds and the slippery slimy mess from inside the pumpkin and then Mommy took a small butcher knife and carefully helped Marie carve a jack-o-lantern face. Darlene pulled open a drawer and fished around among odds and ends of assorted things until she found the stub of an old candle and then she secured it inside the pumpkin.

When it grew dark on Saturday evening (which was really Halloween night,) Mommy lit the candle inside the pumpkin. Grandpo and Grandmo came over from their house to admire the jack-o-lantern and Mommy poured everyone a little glass of apple cider. The cider came in a clear glass jug that was shaped like a pumpkin.

Donald took a sip of his cider and let out a contended sigh, "Honey," that's what he often called Darlene, "Honey" he said, "that's damned good stuff."

Marie gulped that cold cider down as fast as she could and asked for more. Mommy cautioned, "Don't drink it so fast. You can't have too much, or you'll make yourself sick."

Grandmo laughed and added, "You'll never want apple cider again, if you get sick on it."

And that evening was the end of innocence at the Simms ranch when it came to the matter of celebrating fun little holidays like Halloween.

Halloween was followed by Thanksgiving.

Grandmo and Grandpo had bought a new car, a Frazier. It was a very comfortable car to ride in with its plush seats that felt just like crushed velvet—not all rubbed off and shiny like the springy seats on Daddy's old Chevy, and having received an invitation from Aunt May they decided to drive up to Portland to Aunt May's and Uncle Elmer's house for Thanksgiving.

Aunt May and Uncle Elmer didn't really live in Portland, they lived in a suburb of Portland called Lake Oswego. They lived in one side of a duplex and their daughter, Ferne, her husband, Relph and their little boy, whose name was Billy, lived on the other side. Billy was Marie's second cousin, and even though he was two years younger it was fun to be with a cousin and they had a good time together. Everything about Aunt May's and Ferne's home was modern and up-to-date and even though Marie's bed was an army cot that Mommy had folded up and stuck in the trunk of the car Marie figured that Aunt May's house was about as good as anyone could ever want, and someday she wanted to live in a modern place too.

As they drove over the mountain pass of the northern Cascade Mountain Range they marveled at tall, stately fir trees covered with snow. It was just like a Christmas Card picture. While Daddy drove, Marie began to chatter away about how it was that the pilgrims and the Indians shared the first Thanksgiving and how the pilgrims had sailed across the ocean on the Mayflower. She told her newly discovered story over and over until Donald was rolling his eyes, and Lottie and Lytle nodded off in the back seat.

Finally, Darlene said, "That's enough now, Marie. You've already told us that story three times."

"But Mommy, I love that story."

"And we're glad that you're learning about the pilgrims, but we've heard it enough for today."

Uncle Elmer took it upon himself to enlarge Marie's world even more when he suggested that the day after Thanksgiving, they should drive into downtown Portland to view a grand parade celebrating the opening of the Christmas season. Uncle Elmer had an office on the second floor of a tall building right on the parade route and from there they would have a fine view and be out of the crowd below.

When the parade was over, they went down to the big Meier and Frank department store and looked at magical Christmas displays in huge store-front windows. Marie had never seen such wonders, not even in Klamath Falls. There was speculation in the gaping crowd as to whether or not Meier and Frank had overplayed their hand when they actually put live reindeer in two of their windows displays.

Uncle Elmer declared that their downtown Portland holiday experience wouldn't be complete until they had lunch across the street at Lipman's mezzanine lunch counter and so they all trooped over and waited in line for a table. If Meier and Frank's Christmas decorations could possibly be outdone it was only by Lipman-Wolfe's department store. When they were finally seated, they were beside the rail overlooking the main floor below. Colored lights and live poinsettias graced every spare inch of counters and pedestals. Tinsel and huge glass Christmas tree ornaments, ornaments too big for any ordinary Christmas Tree that Marie had ever seen, were suspended on wires. If it sparkled or glistened it was on display.

Marie ate chicken croquettes. She had never had such a fancy lunch. Aunt May said they had to try Lipman's famous sherbet because it was made especially and only for Lipman's lunch counter. It was good and Grandmo said that she thought it was the best thing she'd ever tasted but silently Marie thought ice cream was better.

On Saturday morning Uncle Elmer suggested that they drive out to where they could see the damage still remaining from the Vanport flood that had wiped out an entire community on the Columbia River last Memorial Day. Marie couldn't understand what she was seeing but the grownups all talked about how awful it was. How suddenly after days of raining away the unusually heavy snow pack from Mt. Hood and the Cascades, the river was swollen beyond capacity until a railroad berm burst with an initial ten feet of water washing suddenly over that entire lowland community. The papers reported that nearly 18,000 people had been left homeless. Although the dykes had been repaired and more dams to assist with flood control were planned there would never be a community of Vanport ever again.

The next day as they drove back over the mountains to Eastern Oregon and the ranch Grandmo and Grandpo and Mommy and Daddy talked about the things they had seen. Lytle said, "First we figured that damnable depression would never end, an' the next thing we knew we had a war on our hands, an' now look at us—we're all livin' high on the hog!"

Lottie answered, "When it's all said and done, it was the war that brought us out of the depression, but it was an awful price to have to pay."

Donald added, "Times are changin' that's for sure; I can hardly believe all this modern stuff an' new inventions every time you turn around. It's got to where a person can't keep up with it."

Marie sat between Grandpo and Grandmo, listening. Darlene marveled over and over about the Christmas decorations, "I've never seen such beautiful displays. I can't imagine the money it'd take to decorate like that. I'm glad I got to see it."

However, years later, when she thought more about it, Marie began to remember that there was one bit of overlooked contention that happened that year and that the whole thing had started with chicken pox. Her entrance into Lake County's public-school system brought communicable childhood diseases home to the Simms Ranch. They knew it was coming. But the timing couldn't have been worse.

She awoke one morning, sick to her stomach, aching and covered with nasty red splotches. It was on Monday—before school let out Friday for Christmas vacation. The best week of school for the entire year!

She missed the Elks' Christmas Tree when all the school children gathered around that giant tree in the middle of the main intersection up town—between the bank, the courthouse, the Mary Jo Shop and the hardware store. After all the Christmas songs had been sung, Santa would come and the men of the Elks Lodge would help Santa pass out bags filled with candy, oranges, apples and nuts.

She missed the Christmas tree that Mrs. Zevely was sure to have decorated for the classroom. The worst part of it all was that she missed the gift exchange between her classmates plus Mrs. Scheidereiter and Mrs. Mercer would bring a wonderful party on the last afternoon of school before Christmas vacation.

While she was in town on Thursday afternoon Darlene went to Mrs. Zevely's room to pick up Marie's home-work assignments and to leave the gift she had wrapped for the student whose name she had drawn. Marie's gift was already beneath the tree and Mrs. Zevely handed it to Darlene.

Mrs. Zevely made a sympathetic clucking and said, "I am so disappointed that Marie has to miss all the fun we are having at school. That darned chicken pox has been making the rounds, however, and she isn't the only student who is out. In fact, there are three others in my classroom home with chicken pox right now. Please tell her how much we miss her."

Marie was excited about her gift. It was a box about six inches square and very, very thin. It was neatly wrapped in shiny foil paper and tied with a prim red ribbon. Prim like the sweet little classmate, Carol Kelso, who had drawn her name. She was delighted when she lifted the lid to find an exquisite little-girl hankie with a painted border of spring bouquets.

Early in the month of January there was an unexpected thaw and mounds of packed snow on the playground melted into puddles of dirty water. During afternoon recess, Carol, no longer her usual sweet self, marched up to Marie with the most indignant glare that Marie had ever encountered. In her hand, dripping with muddy playground water, was Marie's Christmas hankie.

"This is what you think of the present I gave you? How dare you be this careless! Don't you even know any better?"

Marie was horrified. The hankie must have fallen from her coat pocket. She loved that beautiful hankie and she had properly written a nice thank-you note to Carol.

Tears slipped down her red cheeks as she took the hankie back, "I'm sorry Carol. I didn't mean to lose it."

Carol sniffed, "Well, you need to learn how to be more careful with things people give you. You should know better."

The bell rang and afternoon recess was over. Marie hung her head as she trudged back into the classroom.

That night, Mommy held Marie on her lap as she sobbed out the story of what happened that awful afternoon. Mommy cuddled her close and said, "Don't worry about it, but maybe this is a lesson for you to be more careful with your things. Perhaps you should have saved the hankie back and not taken it to school. Carol is a very nice little girl. When she found the hankie in the puddle, I think you hurt her feelings, just like she hurt yours by saying those hateful things to you."

And that was the only blight on the entire year of first grade. Marie did, however, remember the Christmas hankie incident and it was a lesson well-learned until she forgot and was careless all over again.

# A New Decade

Early in the summer of 1950 she celebrated her seventh birthday. The calendar, Grandmo and the census taker who canvased the valley marked the beginning of a new decade.

A ten-year span of time is bound to bring about changes. None of us is given a peek into the future except perhaps for parents as they strive to raise children in the hope of ensuring a bright promise of tomorrow. As it was, there seemed to be no exception to the fact that folks in the valley lived a mostly contented and peaceful life, and at seven Marie was undisturbed by any unforeseen changes lingering on the near horizon of her life.

Her present interest was centered around Daddy's new carpentry project.

Donald and Darlene had decided to build a couple of regular bedrooms onto their house. There was a reason for their decision and we'll get to that part of the story later.

Whatever their reason, Marie was glad. She looked forward to the prospect of sleeping downstairs in a brand spanking new bedroom. It was sure to be bright, airy, full of sunshine and smelling of new paint. A year of school in Mrs. Zevely's classroom decorated with colorful pictures and modern new furniture had awakened Marie's senses to modern. It was probably a given notion already, that she would love light and modern forever. Up until the present, however, she had shared a rather dreary upstairs room with Mommy and Daddy.

Like many another country home during that era their house had begun as one room with additions built on whenever money and time allowed. Donald's and Darlene's one room beginner had once been a bunkhouse built atop the remains of an old rock cellar after a catastrophic fire had demolished a large and fine old house at the ranch beneath the rim. After the fire, that rock cellar had provided a stable foundation for the room where Lytle, Lottie and young Donald had lived until a small cottage across the wide dirt driveway could be readied for them. After they began to live in the little gray house the room above the cellar became a bunkhouse. When Donald and Darlene married in August of 1942, the bunkhouse above the rock cellar became their home. Less than a year later, when Marie was born, it was still home for the young couple.

Donald scrabbled money together during the summer of 1943 and by fall he had enough to buy lumber from Emil Hartig's sawmill up on Moss Creek.

He built a large room on the ground level, snugged up against the rock cellar, and connected it to the room above with an enclosed stairway. He made a partition across the room and the south half became the front room and the north half was the kitchen. Eventually he built a back porch off the kitchen and with a lean-to woodshed propped against the north side of the rock cellar they had had an adequate and substantial home for the first seven years of Marie's life.

The room above the cellar then served as one long bedroom for all three: Donald, Darlene and Marie.

There was a nice window in the front part where Mommy and Daddy slept and a doorway that opened to an outside porch. Marie's bed was in the back part near the stairway and discreetly behind a partial partition.

And that was the problem. Marie's bedtime was promptly at eight o'clock. She was scared to go to bed, all alone, in that dark room. Hanging on the wall above her bed was a picture of a huge, shaggy, buffalo head with a halo of horns that looked precisely like those of the devil himself. Marie squeezed her eyes shut, doing her best to pretend that the picture wasn't there. But through her closed eyes she felt those beady, black eyes staring down—right at her. One time they had taken a road trip through Yellowstone Park. She had seen buffalo. She knew first-hand how big, ugly and fearsome they were.

"Mommy," she cried out.

Donald and Darlene were dutiful about their task of raising a disciplined, unspoiled child. Their main reason, perhaps, was due to the fact that there was a set of doting grandparents who lived less than a mediocre stone's throw across the dirt road.

Daddy heard her whimpering and yelled up the stairs, "Oh for God's sake – it's just a picture! Turn over, and go to sleep."

But Mommy came upstairs anyway, tucked the covers closer around her little daughter and soothed, "It's alright, sweetheart. I'll leave the door open a crack."

Her courage was bolstered somewhat by the sliver of light that slid up the stairway. But out of the corner of her eye she could still see that ugly buffalo head staring down as he cast his evil, beady eyes upon her.

During the summer, her eight o'clock bedtime was eased off a bit, but when school started, she had to go to bed, once again, precisely at eight o'clock. During the summer between first grade and second grade Mommy, Daddy and Marie had discovered a new radio program called "Beulah" and "Beulah" came on Monday through Friday at eight o'clock.

As soon as the local and national news and the weather report were over, radio waves were crammed with entertaining programs. Westerns, mysteries, dramas, musical programs, and comedies. "Fibber Magee and Molly" and "Father Knows Best" were on for a half-hour and then it was time for "Beulah."

Beulah was the maid, housekeeper and cook for an up-and-coming young couple in a made-up city located somewhere in the midst of the United States. The program was so cleverly cast that no one had to describe her. Right away everyone could tell that Beulah was a plump, middle-aged, black woman. She had a delightful accent and she said hilarious things. There was always some outrageous problem in the young couple's household, but between the husband and wife and Beulah they figured out a way to resolve every problem and everyone laughed till their sides split. It was an ageless program meant for young and old alike.

Daddy was strict and grumpy about the buffalo picture incidents and he cast a dutiful frown in Mommy's direction when she left the stairway door open, but when "Beulah" came on, he marched right over to the radio and turned it up extra loud. The laughter banished the notion of the ugly buffalo head, and after "Beulah" the next thing Marie knew was Mommy shaking her to get up and get ready for school.

During the summer of 1950 Donald and Lytle used every spare bit of time they could find to tear down the empty house up on the Kimzey place. The house was located up the hill from the barn about a quarter-mile. Donald had bought the little homestead from Bill and Clara Kimzey when they decided to retire and move into town.

The Kimzey place had been a hard-luck little homestead that had gradually become surrounded by the Simms Ranch as Lytle and Lottie had purchased various pieces of land. There had always been a friendly coexistence with Bill and Clara living just up the hill a piece because Bill often worked for them as a sheepherder or milked cows or whatever else needed an extra hand around the ranch. Clara usually cooked for the Hotchkiss ranch down at the end of Abert Lake.

They were careful as they took the Kimzey house down, piece by piece, because Donald intended to use the lumber for those new bedrooms.

When nothing was left but the floor Donald sawed the floor into two sections. He jacked up the sections and put log skids underneath. Early Sunday morning he harnessed Dolly and Prince, led them up the hill and hitched them to the skids. Prince and Dolly were used to work in the hayfields so dragging the skids downhill was an easy pull for them.

Donald urged them along and guided them around until the floor was successfully placed over empty fifty-gallon gasoline drums that he had already positioned behind the kitchen and front room—about where he wanted the floor section. That afternoon he did the same thing with the second section of floor.

When Marie saw those fine smooth sections of flooring, she wanted to jump on them and run around but Daddy said, "No. You stay off of it until I get them where I want an' fastened down good."

It didn't take that long, but to Marie it seemed like once Daddy quit the hayfield for the day, he spent evening after evening rolling the pieces of floor around on the barrels until he had them positioned just where it suited him and Mommy. Finally, one evening he had the floors fastened securely together. He told Marie that she could run and play on them during the day while he worked in the hayfield, but when he was sawing, fitting and nailing she had to stay out of his way.

She galloped her stick horses across the floor. She shouted and yelled, "Hi Ho Silver, Away!" And, "Get 'em up Scout!"

Those smooth empty floors were a fine place to play, but it didn't take long until Daddy began to frame the walls and build a partition and that was the end of that. Evening after evening the bedrooms and a hallway to connect them to the front room began to take shape.

There were times during that summer when Donald put the bedroom project on hold while he and Lytle went down to work on a new addition to the grange hall.

Earlier that year, back during the cold, blustery days of March the Valley Falls Grange was organized. For weeks, and maybe even months, the adults of the valley talked over the pros and cons of organizing a grange. Some thought it was a swell idea because the state grange and the national grange had influence over the agricultural interests of the country. Others, however, thought that they just ought to organize a community club of some sort. It was a well-known fact that other granges in the county were famous for potlucks and dances. Why did they need an organization for that?

She didn't pay a lot of attention to what they were talking about, but Marie would often walk into Grandmo's house to find her standing with one elbow braced on the wooden shelf of the crank telephone as she talked with Vesta Bean, Aunt Leona or sometimes Bessie Carroll about this new idea of organizing a grange. There was no telephone over at their house so she never heard Mommy talking about the grange to anyone except maybe Daddy at supper, or perhaps Grandmo when she brought over some news or the newspaper.

Mainly it was Harry Reed, who with his wife, Emma, lived during their retirement in a little house down by the store and Pat Passage, who had bought the Chandler Station Ranch from Aunt Ottie and Uncle George Chandler who influenced the thinking of folks in the valley and convinced them that an organized grange was the way to go.

One Saturday evening folks in the valley packed the kids in their cars along with pies, cakes, and sandwiches. When Marie asked Mommy what the sudden hustle and bustle was all about Mommy answered, "We're all going over to the station tonight. People have come down from the Oregon State Grange, over in Salem, and we're going to organize a grange right here in Valley Falls. Won't that be fun?"

"Yes."

She didn't know whether it would be fun or not but if Mommy said so it must be true. Mommy was right about most things.

By the end of March, after the second grange meetings had been held, everyone knew that the grange was going to be a whole lot of fun and even folks from town were ready to join.

As soon as the meeting was over Aunt Lora began to play the piano and the grownups danced. The house over at the station had a good-sized open stairway and mothers filled plates of food for their kids and placed them out of the way on those stairs. It was somewhat tricky to keep a plate of food balanced on your lap, but other than that the stairway turned out to be a perfect place to watch everything going on below.

When word about the dancing and potlucks spread to the far corners of the valley, Crooked Creek Valley, into Lakeview and even up toward Paisley the demand for membership began to explode beyond the original expectations of even Harry Reed and Pat Passage. There was, of course, the intent of leverage through grange lobbyists for better agricultural measures and then folks found out that the Oregon State Grange had a good and reasonable insurance program, but the real drawing card was good old-fashioned country fun.

Right away it was obvious that a meeting hall was paramount.

Grandpo, who was Lytle Simms, Vest Carroll, and Harry Reed struck an easy deal with the local school district to buy the old Valley Falls schoolhouse for use as a community hall where the grange could meet.

Grandpo laughed about the proceedings when he came home from the lawyer's office in town. He told Grandmo and Mommy and Daddy all about it during supper over at Grandmo's house that night.

"Well," he said, "as soon as we convinced the school board that that old building isn't worth a plugged nickel, each one of us put up a dollar bill an' the deal was done. One thing's for sure, it's been sittin' there empty for so damned long, it's gonna take a lot of work to get it fixed up, but with everyone pitchin' it won't take that long, either."

Feeling more than a little responsible for the whole proceeding, Donald and Lytle Simms wanted to do their fair share of the work. That fall, even though Donald hadn't finished his work on their new bedrooms, he spent most of his Saturdays and Sundays working on the grange hall. Men came out from town to work on the building as well as those in the valley and the whole building project turned into jolly good times. At least in the eyes of the kids who had to tag along on those work days.

The men used cement blocks as they constructed a long addition for a meeting hall onto the east side of the old schoolhouse. While the men were busy with their work, the women cleaned and worked on the old part of the building as they converted it into a dining room with long tables and set out a hearty potluck meal at noontime. In the meantime, kids tore around playing hide and seek through the cheat grass and behind tall sagebrush. When they grew tired of that they meandered down to the bridge over Crooked Creek where they dragged sticks through the mud and splashed at bugs skating around on the scummy fall water.

But just as soon as he was done with harvesting the grain Donald began to work all day, almost every day, on the new bedrooms. He wanted them done before the snow began to fly.

One Saturday morning Mommy lingered at the breakfast table with Marie.

"Marie" she said, "I want to tell you something."

"What Mommy."

"Sometime, just before Christmas, there will be a baby brother or maybe a baby sister for you!"

Her eyes widened. Suddenly this was quite interesting, "There will?"

"Yes. This afternoon, Grandmo and you and me, well we are all going to a party down at the grange hall. The grange ladies, the Home Ec. Club, are having a shower for our new baby."

"What's a shower, Mommy?"

"It's a party where everyone brings a present for the new baby. There will be all sorts of beautiful things that we'll use for your new little brother or sister."

Darlene continued with emphatic instructions, "Now I want you to take a bath this morning. This afternoon we'll get dressed up nice an' go down to the grange hall for the baby shower."

"Well," Marie thought to herself, "I'm going to get a baby brother!"

Although Mommy had cautioned differently, she didn't even consider a sister. She had instantly brushed that idea aside because she already had it figured out that the new baby was going to be a boy.

"My oh my," it suddenly came to her mind, "I want a baby brother more than anything in the whole wide world!"

# An Angel at the South School

When school had started that fall those new bedrooms were still a work in progress.

It was set in stone that on the first Tuesday morning of September Lake County schools began. No matter how tired, groggy and grumpy children were from one last ride on the merry-go-round, Ferris Wheel or one last (please, please, puuleeezz) cotton candy or candied apple as the annual Labor Day Fair and Round-up came to its glorious close, Lake County students went back to school.

Tuesday morning found round-up flags limp and hamburger stands looking the worse for wear as they waited their turn to come down. Trash littered sleepy streets and blew about here and there into dirt filled corners along Lakeview's tired downtown.

However, Vest Carroll had the school bus shiny clean and ready for a new year and all seemed well as it ground to a stop by the front steps of the North School. Vest grabbed the lever and opened the door. Mrs. Barry was waiting for them and rushed to intercept the arriving students.

"Vest" she said, "there's been a change of plans. Mr. Ferrin, the superintendent, just called me and Valley Falls students are to be sent down to the South School. Jenny is waiting for them."

"Well, alright."

Vest shut the door, put the bus in gear and drove on across town to the South School. Marie, Madge and Mike were dumbfounded and a little scared. They had expected their lives to be a smooth continuation of last year with the only change being that they had advanced a year and would now be in second grade.

Miss Jenny Carroll, by reputation the infamous principal down at Lakeview's South School, waited with a definite air of impatience. She was the exact opposite of the no-nonsense yet happy-go-lucky Mrs. Laura Barry, principal and matriarch of Lakeview's North School.

Miss Carroll squinted into the rising eastern sun. Gentle September breezes knew better than to ruffle her red hair. Her dress and shoes were spartan, prim and proper. She was a small person, by stature, but outward appearances were deceiving because there was nothing soft nor demure about her. Her lips were pursed tight.

"Good morning, Vest. I see you got the message."

She tried to force a smile as she approached the bus. Already on this very first morning of a brand-new school year, as far as Jenny Carroll was concerned, nothing was going the way it should.

"Good morning, Jenny."

Vest attempted to make his voice cheerful as he motioned for his young charges to come forward and step down. Vest Carroll knew Miss Jenny Carroll quite well because, odd as it seemed, knowing the two of them, Miss Carroll was actually Vest's sister.

The high school students, mainly the boys, snickered among themselves. "Those poor little devils—they sure as hell don't know what they're in for."

Not only that, it turned out that that evening out at the Simms ranch, the events of that fateful day created a rather lively discussion.

Mommy said, "Marie, it's not nice to call someone an 'Old Maid.' She's a spinster. We only say 'Old Maid' when we play your card game."

"What's a spin …. uh … spinster, Mommy?"

Daddy was quick. "It's an ornery old biddy that couldn't find a man dumb enough or gullible enough to marry her."

Grandmo put in, "Donald! Donald! Don't talk that way!"

Grandpo knew when to keep his mouth shut.

No one in Marie's family, most of all Daddy, was happy about her being transferred down to the South School

As they stepped down from the bus that first morning Miss Carroll had issued a crisp command, "Follow me."

Instinct told them to march and to march silently. Up the front steps, through the front door, up a short flight of wooden stairs, sharp left turn into the hallway where the smell of newly polished wood still lingered.

"Mike Counts—you are in Mrs. Moffit's room." She motioned left.

"Madge Schofield and Marie Simms—you are in Mrs. Greene's room." She motioned right.

They entered the room. They looked up at Mrs. Greene. She was a taller, stouter version of Miss Carroll.

Students already in their seats only stared as Mrs. Greene ushered these two new country girls to their desks—they dare not smile. Their seats were the last two empty desks at the end of five rows of wooden desks fastened together with black wrought iron. Those desks were foreign, stiff and unfriendly. Nothing was like the North School.

During recess the other girls tried to make friends with them. Marie felt so scared and quivery inside that she could hardly talk. There was one almost good thing. Her first cousin, Iney—Inez Icenhower, Aunt Wilma's daughter, went to the South School. And Iney was a veteran from having served there during first grade.

Iney and Marie were almost the exact same age. She had been gifted with thick, bouncy, curly red hair. Mommy said that Iney sure didn't get that hair from Aunt Wilma, who was Mommy's sister—that it must have come from the Icenhower side. Iney lived in town and her way of life was miles apart from Marie's country life and although the two girls were well acquainted, they didn't see each other very often.

Iney tried to be friendly with Marie but she was tugged away by another red headed cousin from over on the Icenhower side of her family. Audrey Icenhower wanted nothing to do with that strange little country girl who acted shy and had ugly, brown braids. Who was she, anyway, this new girl who had suddenly turned up in their territory down at the South School?

Bad as everything else was, the worst part of that day was lunch. Up at the North School there was a lunchroom in the basement, and hot lunch was brought up from the high school, but there was no lunchroom down at the South School. Most of the South School kids went home for lunch. Those who ate at school had to run two blocks up H street to the high school cafeteria.

Marie wanted to give up and not even try to eat lunch that day, but Madge was bolder and braver and she convinced Marie that they ought to give it a try. Madge grabbed Marie's hand and tugged until she gave up and ran up the street to the high school.

Marie envied Madge and figured that Madge could do anything that she set her mind to. Madge was gifted with long slim legs and she was far more athletic than Marie. She had older brothers and sisters who taught her how to do many things. On Sundays the Schofield family drove into Lakeview and went to church. In Marie's eyes, Madge oozed confidence and bravery, her hair was blonde and she had pretty blue eyes.

Marie, on the other hand, was short, round and rather awkward. Her hair, although it lay in thick rich braids, was brown, but her eyes were not beautiful brown.

Mommy tried to console Marie, "Well they call the color of your eyes hazel."

Marie wished that her eyes would at least have been brown if they could not be blue, or maybe even green.

They ran as fast as they could. Because it was only the first day of school, the high school kids were still in the mood to put on their best behavior and so they stood back to let the grade-school kids go to the head of the line. Marie and Madge wisely chose a seat at the far end of the furthermost table. They gulped their food as fast as they could swallow. They ran back to the school as fast as they could. There was no time to spare and they made it just in time for the bell to ring for afternoon class.

And that was the first day of second grade.

Grandpo picked her up at the store that evening. If it had been either Daddy or Grandmo, Marie might have been able to muster a stiff upper lip but when she saw Grandpo, tears of despair began to trickle down her cheeks. Grandpo was, after all, her best protector.

Lottie, upon hearing the pickup, glanced out the front room window and when she saw Lytle take Marie by the hand and lead her into Donald's and Darlene's house, she sensed that something was wrong. She hastened out the front door and scurried across.

Darlene was helping Donald hang sheet rock in the new bedrooms and when Grandpo hollered out, "We've got a mighty troubled little girl here," they emerged from their carpentry project.

Daddy took the nails out of his mouth and laid them on the table beside the hammer. Marie rushed to Mommy and as Darlene plumped down in the nearest chair, she gathered her into her softness. Marie began to sob out the story of that terrible day.

Donald began to swear and rant and rave.

Lottie tried to calm the storm, "Now Donald. Jenny Carroll taught you during your second year of school."

"You 're damned right she did, an' I swore up an' down that that ol' rip would never teach any of my kids!"

Darlene tried to soothe, "She's only the principal, Donald, Edith Greene is her teacher."

"I'm scared of Mrs. Greene, Mommy. I don't think she likes me!"

Darlene sighed, "I'll see Wilma next time we're in town and see what she has to say. Iney goes to the South School."

Marie continued to sob into Mommy's lap, "I…. Iney doesn't like me ei…. either."

Grandpo, being the wise man that he was, turned and walked out the front door. Grandmo heaved a sigh and followed.

Nothing improved. Marie trembled through each day. Her only relief came when she boarded the school bus and headed for home. When Mommy saw Aunt Wilma, Aunt Wilma said, "Well we've got no choice. Iney has to go to the South School. She doesn't like school very much. Course that's where all Iney's friends go. Marie needs to toughen up like the rest of the kids."

Daddy liked to tease Aunt Wilma. He said that she had lived in the south end of town so long that she had traded her midwestern South Dakota drawl for a southern Arkie twang.

One Friday Mrs. Schofield checked Madge out of school. They were going to spend the winter in California. Marie's heart sank. Her last fortress of support had fallen.

On Monday morning right after recess Mrs. Greene announced, "Take out your paper and pencils, it's time for a spelling test."

Mrs. Greene stood at the front of the room and enunciated each word with distinct care. Marie was careful to be neat as she printed her spelling words. Her eyes drifted across the aisle. There sat Jerretta Baker writing her words in beautiful long hand.

"Marie Simms! Put down your pencil and come to the front of the room!"

Terrified, she looked up! Her face grew red as she walked to the front.

"There! You sit on the floor with your face to the wall. We do NOT tolerate cheating at this school."

"I …. I was only looking at her writing. I don't know how to write."

"Sit! Do not talk back to me!"

Her face grew redder and redder. She bit her bottom lip to keep from crying as she sat with her legs folded on the floor. She dared not drop her weary head into her aching arms. Mrs. Greene hated her. She knew it. It was a very sore point with Mrs. Greene, (had she not said so many times?) that the North School did not teach long hand in the first grade.

She was forced to sit on the floor, getting further and further behind in her schoolwork, until, at last, the bell rang for yet another unmerciful lunch hour.

By this late date in the school year, the high school students were not inclined to be polite. If the teacher on lunch room duty was not paying attention, as was often the case, they would tease and not let the grade-school kids go to the front of the line. What difference did it make? She was too terrified and sick at her stomach to eat, anyway. She would never make it back in time.

And she was right. She did not.

As she raced into the school yard, Miss Carroll, who, as fate would have it, was taking her turn at playground duty, caught her by the coat collar.

"Marie Simms! You are late! March inside this minute!"

Miss Carroll held her collar as they marched through the door and up the stairs and then shoved her down on the top step.

"You may sit right there until I tell you to do different."

She wheeled around and marched on down the hall. Even the sound of her footsteps was steeped in exasperation.

Marie could take no more. She was at the bottom of despair. She didn't care that the stairs were no longer polished and clean, but dirty and caked with dried mud from trip after trip by hordes of children as they hurried to and from the playground. So what if her clothes got filthy as she sat there? She dropped her head into her arms and her whole body began to shake with sobs.

"My dear little girl, whatever is troubling you so?"

It was an incredibly sweet voice—the nicest and softest voice Marie had ever heard.

She looked up. Sitting beside her was a ray of sunshine. The kindest woman she had ever seen in her entire life. That sweet personage put her arm around Marie and as Marie gazed into that angel face, she sobbed out the entire miserable story.

"Well Marie Simms, I am Mrs. Moffit. I teach second grade. I know who you are because Mike Counts is in my room."

Then she took Marie's hand, "Come with me little girl. Let's see what I can do."

She led Marie into her classroom. She took out tissues and wiped Marie's face and hands and sat her at a desk.

"You wait here while I visit with Miss Carroll."

And so, it turned out that the angel teacher took Marie into her own classroom. In the hours after school while they waited for the school bus to arrive from the high school, she taught Marie and Mike how to write in longhand.

Gratitude abounded for Mrs. Moffit. Not only from Marie, herself, but also from Mommy and Daddy, and Grandpo and Grandmo. In truth of the matter, Miss Jenny Carroll must also have been grateful for the angel teacher. A teacher with patience—a quality that she had never been able to master—nor had Mrs. Greene, and it is quite likely that Mrs. Greene was as grateful as everyone else.

# Waiting for Raymond George

Bernice Moffit brought light and life back into Marie's education—limited as it was so far. Very little of life's difficulties had entered her awareness up until those beginning days of second grade, and no doubt it was the reason that she always remembered those excruciating days between the first week of September through mid-November when Mrs. Moffit found her sobbing on the mud-covered stairway down at the South School. Over the years whenever Marie's thoughts turned to guardian angels, she immediately remembered Bernice Moffit.

The truth of the matter was that in spite of her suffering at school the rest of her world kept on turning quite nicely. Mommy was deeply involved with the approaching birth of her baby and Daddy used every extra minute he could find to put the finishing touches on their new bedrooms.

Darlene's baby was due sometime after the first week in December.

As she waited for the bedrooms to be completed, Darlene spread all the beautiful new baby clothes, blankets and miscellaneous finery out an old divan in the front room. Divan is an old-fashioned word that describes a couch or a sofa. A piece of furniture that could possibly become a make-shift bed if there was no other place to bed down unexpected guests.

The divan, shoved into one corner, was seldom used in the waning days of 1950 because no matter from what angle you looked at it, it was as ugly and uncomfortable as any piece of furniture ever made. The dull black horsehair upholstery was rough, cold and sewed into triangular tuffs. It curved up at one end and had long since gone out of style. The only thing it was good for in those days was to hold odds and ends of stuff that somehow, in spite of our best efforts, accumulate and have the need to be stacked somewhere out of the way. Darlene cleaned off the collection of outdated magazines and newspapers and spread out the fast-accumulating baby finery.

Marie and Darlene had taken to spending their spare time admiring those baby things. One by one they picked up each little gown, receiving blanket and crocheted shawl. Darlene made sure that Marie's hands weren't covered with sticky residue and that her own hands were perfectly clean before they ran their hands over the softness, picked up each item and brushed it against their cheeks.

They could hardly wait—the mother to hold her baby and the sister to play with her new baby brother. Marie had no concept of the fact that it would take several years before he would grow into a suitable playmate and thus provide the companionship for which she longed. Nor did she have a concept of the age difference that, as children, would always exist between the two of them.

She let out a soft sigh and said, "I can hardly wait to see my baby brother."

"It won't be long now," Mommy said, "but sweetheart remember, it might be a little sister, not a brother."

"I know," she answered, but down deep inside she knew it was a brother. No one could convince her otherwise.

Meanwhile, over at her house, Lottie was busy crocheting rag rugs for the new bedrooms.

She had a rather peculiar room in her house that was located between the dinette and front room. Dinette is another old-fashioned word meaning that the room was too small to be considered a regular dining room but on the other hand it adequately held an informal dining table and chairs—in Grandmo's case a modern chrome set with light grey laminate.

Lottie was proud of that dinette with her fancy new table and chairs, and those having meals at her house no longer had to be underfoot as they squeezed into her kitchen with its strangely uneven floor.

The little room off the dinette would have been akin to a central hall if only it had been in the center of the house—but it wasn't. In truth it was not large enough to be considered an actual room. A treadle-style Singer sewing machine sat against one wall under a pitiful window. The window was so small that even on the brightest of summer days it let in very little sunlight. A chest of drawers, its top overflowing with odds and ends of assorted items, put there mostly by Lytle, sat against another partial wall. Messy as the top was, the drawers were full of neatly ironed and orderly arranged kitchen linens. The opposite wall was covered with hooks and nails on which an assortment of coats and jackets were hung. Another door opened from that same wall into an enormous closet.

It was really a walk-in closet but everyone simply referred to it as "Grandmo's closet." In truth of the matter, it was not possible to walk more than a couple of steps into the closet because it was full—massively full—full to overflowing. Treasures from the past were forever buried in there as well as items that were bound to come in handy. To give Lottie credit, the stuff that was actually used from time to time was conveniently stored just inside the door.

Marie loved her grandmother's closet; she loved to poke and pry through all that stuff, but possibly the most fascinating and informative item was Grandmo's big doctor book. Whenever a little-known ailment or outbreak occurred, not only to the Simms family, but also to others who lived in the valley Grandmo consulted the doctor book.

It could be said that Grandmo's doctor book provided more information than even Grandmo was ever made aware, because there were anatomically correct pictures of both the female and male nude bodies in that book. Marie and her cousin, Sharon, could situate themselves quite comfortably among piles of soft old junk as they studied the book. Sharon did have a younger brother, but Marie had yet to gaze upon a naked male body.

Lottie kept her scrap bags in that closet. She had never knowingly discarded a piece of usable fabric. Worn, outdated, faded and ripped pieces of clothing as well as the ends of old blankets were stuffed into those scrap bags. During the summer of the new bedrooms, she began to sort through her scrap bags to ferret out suitable material for rag rugs that would complement the linoleum planned for each bedroom floor.

"Marie," she said, "what color would you like for your room?"

When Marie answered that her favorite color was red, Grandmo said, "Well that's a nice color but wouldn't you rather sleep in a room that's more pink than red?"

"I guess."

The color of her room didn't bother her much as long as it was downstairs and that ugly buffalo head picture with his evil beady eyes wasn't staring down at her every night.

Lottie didn't bother to ask an opinion on the color for Darlene's and Donald's room because she knew that Donald's favorite color was blue and Darlene went along with whatever Donald liked.

She began to cut and sew long strips of fabric together. She used a giant wooden crochet hook as she crocheted the strips into two lovely oblong rugs.

While Grandmo crocheted, Marie spent contended hours close to her side as she worked on her scrapbook. Aunt May Ashlstrom and Aunt May's daughter, Ferne, made a gift of the scrapbook to her on her seventh birthday. It was huge. It was half as big as Marie was tall. The cover was a soft brown tweedy material bound with a luxurious silken tassel.

With the book came an assortment of colorful magazines. Hour after hour she sat cross-legged on Grandmo's front room rug while she selected pictures. She used Grandmo's sewing scissors as with painstaking care she cut out a picture. Lottie winced when she looked up from her crocheting to see Marie slather on paste with wide generous strokes, but then Marie would carefully place the picture just so onto a page.

Darlene, herself, was not in the least disappointed that Marie kept that scrapbook project over at Lottie's house. While Lottie crocheted and Marie cut and pasted, they had great conversations about the pictures and anything else that happened to come to their minds.

Marie was delighted whenever she happened upon a picture of five special little girls. Their black hair lay in lovely ringlets, their cheeks were rosy red and they were always dressed in identical dresses.

"Grandmo, do you know who these little girls are? They're in lots an' lots of magazines."

"Those are the Dionne Quintuplets. They're five sisters all born at the same time. You know, like there are twins sometimes. Instead of two, there are five of them. Everyone admires them because they're a medical marvel and aren't they just the cutest little things? They live up in Canada. They're in all the advertisements for Karo syrup."

"Wow! They sure have pretty clothes. I wish I could have dresses like that."

Lottie replied, "Don't be so envious of them. I read where some folks think they've been taken advantage of by all those big companies who want to use them for advertisement. Of course, they're being paid a lot of money for that. People who claim to know what they are talking about accuse their father of taking the money for himself and not properly putting it away for them when they grow up. I guess the one little girl is not as healthy as they make her up to be in those pictures."

"Ummmm. Well, I like them. I don't know which I like best, them or Elsie the Cow, an' Elmer the Bull an' their calf, Junior. They're funny," Marie giggled.

"Yes, they're owned by Carnation Milk Company. I think maybe those made-up characters are better used."

Marie turned a few more pages, "What about Hopalong Cassidy? He isn't made-up, is he, Grandmo?"

"Well, yes and no. He's a real man, but he's an actor who plays a made-up character. The Dairy Farmers and any company that can get ahold of that character sure like to use him in their ads. It's all for money and big business. Someday you'll understand. For now, just enjoy the pictures and put them in your scrapbook."

When the fall of the year had waned and the trees stood bare of their last golden leaves, but just before serious snow began to fall, Donald put away his nails and his hammer and cleaned the last paintbrush. The bedrooms were done.

Everything in Marie's room was in a shade of pink. Pink flowers were in the curtains at the windows and pink flowers were in a curtain hung over the closet door. A pink chenille bedspread was spread on her new wooden spindle bed. Pink swirls in the smooth linoleum floor were topped with Grandmo's crocheted rug in hues ranging from dark red, to mauve and to rosy pink.

It would be nice to say that she always kept that wonderful new bedroom neat, the toys and clothes picked up and her bed made. But the truth of the matter is that she did not.

Darlene's and Donald's room was slightly the larger of the two. As Marie's bedroom was decorated in pink, theirs was decorated in shades of blue. Except for one thing—in the corner, over by Mommy's side of the bed, stood a baby crib—waiting for Marie's new baby brother or perhaps baby sister. It was the same crib that was used when Marie was born. It was made of cast iron entwined with a filigree made to look like rose buds, and it was painted with durable high-gloss enamel in a Pepto-Bismol shade of pink.

"Oh well," she sighed to herself, "I guess my little brother won't mind using my old pink crib."

By the second week in December the winds howled every night through the naked branches of the old Poplar trees and snow began to fall.

One morning at breakfast Darlene's voice had a slight worried tone, "Seems like this winter's bound to be hard. I wonder how long this storm's going to last."

Donald answered, "Don't worry. That jeep pickup we got last winter doesn't let much get in its way, an' besides that, I put the blade on the tractor yesterday. We'll make it out just fine."

Two mornings later, Mommy woke Marie a little earlier than usual. She was already dressed for going to town and so was Daddy. There was hot mush on the table, and toast, but Mommy and Daddy didn't eat any of it.

"Alright, Sister," that's what Daddy had taken to calling her sometimes now, "hurry up. Have you got everything you need for school?

Daddy seemed to be in charge of things this morning.

Lottie was there too. When Donald rushed Darlene and Marie out the door, she turned from the kitchen sink to holler over her shoulder, "Don't worry. Dad an' I'll take care of everything out here. Don't forget to call us when you know something."

They got into Grandpo's and Grandmo's good car instead of the pickup. Grandpo had backed it out of the garage, and it was already cozy and warm.

At the store, Daddy let her out and told her to ride the school bus—just like always. She was in a daze. Nothing about this morning was normal but instinct told her not to ask any questions.

Once she was on the bus with the other kids, it was easy to forget most of the turmoil at home, but still in times of lull when she should have been studying, she wondered and worried.

When the last bell of the day rang, she was surprised when she looked up and saw Daddy walk through the door.

He was polite to Mrs. Moffit and then he said to Marie, "Come with me. Mrs. Moffit'll let Vest know that you won't be on the bus tonight."

Mommy was not waiting in the car and as soon as he shut the door he turned to Marie with a big grin and said, "Well Sister, you were right. You have a baby brother. He and Mommy 'll have to stay in the hospital for a few days."

Right after the Pledge of Allegiance the next morning, Mrs. Moffit said, "Marie has an announcement this morning. Come to the front and tell us your good news."

In her usual state she would have ducked her head and been too shy, but on that particular morning she was bursting with happiness. Unbeknownst to her how she managed to do it, she was propelled to her feet with a courage she usually lacked.

"I have a new baby brother. He was born yesterday afternoon and his name is Raymond George."

As her classmates gasped, and smiled and clapped, her face grew beet red and she almost ran back to her seat.

# Remembering Grandpa Brown

Once Christmas break was over there was a new kind of excitement. During Christmas vacation first and second grade classrooms were moved into a brand-new addition down at the South School. An identical addition had also been built up at the North School. During the first days of January all that newness made concentration on lessons a little hard. Time, however, intervened and once again routine was established.

Those rooms were as modern as modern could be had during the end of 1950 and the beginning of 1951. The cabinetry and desks were all done in honey-blonde tones of wood. The windows were expansive in width and tall clear to the ceiling. It's possible that the windows had not been well thought out, because during the spring when the sun moved to the north thick draperies were ordered and hung to block out the sun's brilliance that blasted heat into those north-facing rooms.

Floor-to-ceiling cupboards were built across the end of each classroom and the lower cabinets were outfitted with sinks and water fountains. It was a modern idea of classrooms that were designed to accommodate small children who dabbled in water colors and paste mixed with playground dirt and a parched thirst brought on by ball games and gymnastics during recess.

Lakeview's school system moved along with the time.

Talk around the dinner table over at Grandmo's house on New Year's Day drifted to the topic of those new additions and the burgeoning population of school-age children.

Lytle leaned back in his chair while he stirred sugar and cream into his second cup of coffee. "Well, it's a fact that things are boomin' all over the country."

Donald was cautious, "This new bond measure they're puttin' on the ballot is sure as hell gonna raise our taxes. The school board thinks we need a whole new school building, now, just for 4th, 5th, and 6th graders."

"If it goes through, and it looks like it will," Darlene added, "it'll be done when Marie starts 5th grade."

Lottie put in that she'd read in the paper where they intended to name the new school building after the late Judge, Arthur D. Hay

All that talk sailed over the top of Marie's head. She was happy to be going back to school. School had turned from terror to wonderful now that she was under the care of Mrs. Moffitt and she even had friends who lived in town. Since the excitement of Christmas was over and life with her baby brother had settled into a semblance of normal, she was ready for school once again.

Winter days began to lengthen and the ranch began to blossom into its own version of High Desert spring. Pussy willows appeared on a bush just outside the back door by the ditch where warm soapy water drained from the kitchen sink. Yellow buttercups opened up in protected grassy lots and lambs bucked and played.

Marie's little brother grew like a weed! Everyone raved over how cute he was. "Look at all that dark curly hair! Have you ever seen a baby with so much hair? Especially on a boy! All those beautiful curls."

In Marie's mostly unspoken opinion he was turning out to be a rather boring and tiresome individual. At first, he slept a lot and then he began to cry a lot. Mommy showed her how to push the baby buggy back and forth with a gentle sort of swinging motion and after her arm felt like it was going to break off from all that swinging and pushing, he finally stopped crying and went back to sleep.

Grandmo said, "Now isn't that a good girl. Don't you just love your little brother?"

Marie was beginning to figure out that members of her family were afraid that she wouldn't love her brother or that she would be jealous of all the attention paid to him and that blasted curly hair. But Marie understood, boring and tedious as he was, that that wasn't about to happen. He was her brother, after all, and that was all there was to that.

When he grew old enough to sit in a high-chair and eat he made a general mess of himself and everything around him. He made stinky poop in his diapers and he did it a lot. In fact, he was beginning to show signs that he would eventually grow into a regular mess of a boy.

When spring came the Schofield family returned to Valley Falls from their winter in California and Madge, her most loyal friend in the world, couldn't seem to get enough of oohing and aahing over Raymond.

"Oh Marie, don't you just love him!? Look at that curly hair? Isn't he the cutest thing you've ever seen?!"

To herself, Marie thought, "Well if he lived at your house you might not think he was so cute."

Grandma Brown and Aunt Frankie came to visit that summer. Grandma Brown was Mommy's mother and Aunt Frankie was Mommy's youngest sister. Grandma Brown was a widow, because Grandpa Brown had died during the late summer of 1947.

Marie could not remember that grandfather. She desperately tried to remember something about him, but the only thing that she could ever recall was his funeral. She was really too young to remember much about that, but over the years she tried to retain memories and what she had been told about him by others. It was a sadness to her that his funeral was the only connection she ever had to that grandfather. She was so much in love with her grandfather Simms that as she grew older it seemed to take on more and more importance to her that she ought to be able recall something about her grandfather, Bert Brown.

The grain crop was abundant that summer of 1947 and so it was that Donald had not completed the harvest when Darlene's father, Darrell Albert Brown, passed away. His passing was sudden. He was only fifty-two. It was the last thing anyone expected.

With the last of the wheat still standing in the field it was decided that Donald should stay behind to finish the combining while Lottie and Lytle drove Darlene and Marie over to Cave Junction for Bert's funeral.

They stayed in a motel. She always remembered the motel with amazing clarity because it was called the, "Wish You Well Motel." In her little-girl memory Marie called it the "wishing-well motel" because there a wishing-well in the courtyard. Lytle, who was left to entertain her while Darlene and Lottie finished their feminine preparations for the day, threw pennies into the well and encouraged her to make outrageous wishes.

When Bert died, Grandma and Grandpa Brown lived in a pretty log cabin located a short distance outside the town limits of Cave Junction, Oregon. In front of the cabin was a winding and narrow paved road which intersected beside their cabin with a dirt road. Directly across the dirt road stood a tiny country church. The church was sparkling white and with the log cabin on the other side of the road the whole scene looked like it belonged on a calendar picture or perhaps the cover of a story book. If the church had been brown instead of white it would truly have been the "little brown church in the wildwood."

The "wildwood" because unlike the arid wide-open spaces found in Lake County, the countryside around the church and Grandma and Grandpa Brown's cabin was overrun and choked with oak trees, underbrush of many varieties and prickly blackberry brambles.

Because it was during those busy days of a funeral congregation it seemed to Marie like there was a never-ending stream of grown-up folks with doleful expressions who milled around and in and out of Grandma Brown's cabin. Some would lean down and take Marie's hand or hug her and kiss her and then say something like, "I'm your Aunt Ellen," or, "I'm your Uncle Darrell. You don't remember me, do you?"

There were also a lot of other children she didn't know. Grandmo explained that almost all of them were her cousins—first cousins, in fact. Mommy's sister, Aunt Wilma lived in Lakeview so of course Marie knew her and her cousin Iney, but everyone else was a blur in a sea of names and faces.

It was more than she could take in, and it was true, after all, that Marie was a bit spoiled. At the ranch, with Grandpo and Grandmo Simms, she was their only grandchild, because it was in a time before either of her brothers were born. Grandma Brown and Grandpa Brown had a regular mob of children and grandchildren. At least it seemed that way to Marie.

Instead of joining in with the mob and getting acquainted with her cousins as Grandmo suggested that she ought to do, she was shy and stood back. When she found Grandpo sitting in a chair pushed back against a wall she went over and climbed in his lap.

Grandpa Brown's funeral was held in the little church across the road. Marie didn't remember that part, but Grandmo, her grandmother Simms, told her about it later. Grandpo kept her at the cabin while Grandmo went to the funeral with Mommy.

The cemetery was down the dirt road a short distance and on a steep hillside. When the funeral procession drove through the cemetery's tall iron gate Lytle stopped the car and took Marie's hand as he opened the door and got out. Lottie scooted across to the driver's seat and drove on as she and Darlene followed the procession up the hillside and disappeared over the top. Marie never thought much about it until years later when she figured out that her mother and grandparents had probably wanted to spare her the sight of Grandpa Brown's coffin, the gravesite and perhaps the trauma of seeing her mother's grief.

A manzanita bush grew beside the cemetery gate. While they waited Grandpo eyed the bush and said, "I think I see a limb on that there bush that'll make a mighty fine stick-horse."

He pulled out his pocket knife and with a flip of his wrist he cut off the limb, trimmed it up and indeed it did make a perfect stick-horse.

"That's a red manzanita bush," Lytle said. "They don't grow as big as that over in our part of the country. What are you gonna call your horse?"

Her imagination was limited and she replied, "I'll call him Red Manzanita."

Marie was a fickle child because right away Red Manzanita replaced her willow stick-horse, "Bronco," as her most favorite. She owned a small dirt stable of stick-horses dropped carelessly down just outside the front door. However, if she was in the mood to show off her rodeo cowgirl skills, she immediately picked up Bronco because he was a wild and wooly bucker whereas Red Manzanita was tall, good-looking and very gentle.

Mother Nature and time took their tolls and eventually Red Manzanita dried out and grew brittle. One day a piece of his tail broke off as Marie galloped in a reckless fashion across the lot between the house and the barn. She was devastated. Daddy, who could not stand her crying gathered Red Manzanita's broken pieces and went to the shop. He squinted as positioned the two slender and brittle twigs into the vise. He then scrounged up a piece of baling wire and wound it tightly around the pieces as he successfully grafted Red Manzanita's tail onto the rest of his body.

As time crept on there came a hot summer day when she carelessly laid Red Manzanita down in some tall rye grass while she climbed into the bed of the grain truck to play in the growing piles of golden wheat kernels. When she grew tired of that, she climbed back over the rack and went to pick up Red Manzanita. But she could not find him.

Mommy searched. Grandmo searched. Even Daddy stopped the tractor and shut the combine down, while he searched through the tall rye grass.

But Red Manzanita was gone–she never saw him again.

The day after Bert Brown's funeral, Donald kept a watch out for the dust cloud that would signal his family's return. When he finally saw it, he heaved a sigh of relief and although he probably would never admit it, his heart leapt for joy. To have his family all together in the place where they belonged, at the ranch, was relieved satisfaction.

About the same time that Donald spied the dust cloud Loyd saw it too and he yelled out, "I'm sewin' up the last sack I got here, you wanna quit fer today?"

"Yeah, I'm gonna head up to the house. What do you think? One more day 'll about finish her off?"

Loyd yelled—it was almost impossible to hear over the noise of the combine and tractor, "By noon tomorrow we'll call this job done fer this year; I'll see ya' in the mornin'."

He didn't always do it, but this evening he stopped on the back porch, took off his dusty, chaff-covered overalls, his sweaty shirt and tossed his grease-stained hat in the corner. Darlene was already slicing potatoes into the popping grease of a frying pan, and ham sizzled in another. Donald grabbed a clean towel and proceeded straight to the kitchen sink to wash up.

"Everything go alright?" He asked over his shoulder.

"Yes."

When he figured he was clean enough, he walked up behind Darlene and put his arm about her waist. She turned in his arms and laid her weary head on his shoulder.

"I'm sorry as hell, honey, about your Dad."

Donald liked his father-in-law, Bert Brown. He respected him as one man to another. "Bert was a hard-workin' man," he thought, "doin' the best he could for his family."

Donald knew he might have it wrong, but he always kinda felt like Darlene might have been her father's favorite. Bert was proud of the fact that Darlene had finished high school and he often remarked about what a fine place the ranch was.

"I know you feel bad about it," Darlene answered, "but you couldn't leave the grain and your Dad isn't up to that kind of work anymore. It's alright. I understand."

Donald had known that his wife would say that, even if she didn't like the fact that it wasn't him by her side at her own father's funeral. She'd say she understood—even if she really didn't. He swallowed the knot in his throat.

"Was it awful—the funeral an' all that?"

"No. Well it was, but Mom and Dad, your Mom and Dad, were right there the whole time. I'm just glad it's over."

He gave her one last squeeze. He was feeling a little more sensitive than he usually did and so he turned and padded upstairs to get some clean clothes on before Marie or his folks might happen to come through the front door.

Darlene took a handkerchief out of her apron pocket and wiped her eyes, blew her nose and turned back to the stove.

Not much was spoken about it ever again.

That was all that Marie could ever remember about Grandpa Brown: The Wish You Well Motel, the picture-perfect log cabin across the road from the little white church, and Red Manzanita. And all of that was because of his funeral—she remembered nothing of the man himself.

# The Red Dress

Back in that summer of 1951 when Grandma Brown and Aunt Frankie came to visit Marie acted a little standoffish with her grandmother. Hazel Brown took it in stride because she had a lot of experience with a lot of grandchildren and she remarked to Darlene, "Don't worry yourself so much about it. It's only natural 'cause she really doesn't know me. She'll get used to me in a while."

On the other hand, it was easy, fun and somewhat enlightening to be around Aunt Frankie. Aunt Frankie was young. She acted like she was an original member of the bobby-sox generation and in the know about everything that was the rage in music, movies and all the latest trends of 1951. She made a cuff halfway between her knee and her ankle on her blue jeans and she wore penny loafers. Not used to country ways she washed her hair every day, did it up in pin curls, tied a scarf around it and wore it that way most of the day.

Aunt Frankie even drove down to the Valley Falls Store and bought soda pop. Not for any special reason—but just because she wanted some! She bought a flavor that Marie had never tasted before—cream soda. Right away Marie liked cream soda, especially poured over a scoop of Lakeview Maid ice cream.

When World War II was over Bert and Hazel Brown had moved from Lakeview to Cave Junction and it was about that same time that Grandma "got religion." That's how Daddy put it. He didn't say it in front of his mother-in-law, of course, but Marie heard him telling Mommy that's what he thought about Grandma Brown's praying over food and all. He did manage to behave himself and bowed his head somewhat when she asked a blessing over the food.

Marie had to admit that she found praying over every single meal every single day somewhat odd. So far, her only experience with praying was when Mrs. Schofield prayed over dinners held down at the grange hall. She didn't mind it, but it made her somewhat uncomfortable because she knew that Grandma's praying over food made her parents uneasy and when they didn't think she was listening she heard them argue about it. It wasn't a huge argument, but just the same, it was an argument.

One day Marie asked Grandmo, her grandmother at the ranch, about praying. Grandmo told her that praying was a good thing and that sometimes she even did it herself. Not in front of anyone, just to herself.

Grandmo told her how it was that when Daddy was a baby, she prayed every day that God would allow her to live long enough so that she could raise him to be a grownup man. She told Marie about how the churches in town had a Sunday school and she wished that Marie could go. But they lived way out in the country and they couldn't be running into town every Sunday just to go to church. Marie figured out that maybe Grandmo thought they ought to, but then Grandmo preferred peace in her family and she usually, but not always, kept that thought to herself.

One afternoon Marie was playing on the old grinding wheel that stood in front of the shop. She peddled away fascinated with the whetstone wheel that turned faster and faster the harder and faster she pedaled. Donald was inside the shop getting a sickle-bar ready for the mowing machine. Lytle was trapped in the back section, behind the old forge, when Lottie stomped out to the shop with a stubborn, indignant look which she was capable of mustering up from time to time.

"Donald," she didn't bother to let rage work its way up, it was already front and center, "you've got to stop cussing so much, especially while Hazel's here. It's shameful the way you talk."

"What! You think her ears are so tender she can't take a few cuss words? Don't tell me you think Bert Brown didn't spew out a few damns and hells."

"Takin' the Lord's name in vain. That's what's so awful. You ought to know better 'n that. I tried to teach you, when you were a kid, but I guess it never worked."

Lytle was wanting to jump over the forge and escape, anywhere, maybe the barn, but he couldn't get out. Marie's mouth dropped open, she hated arguments, but at the same time she couldn't make herself run away.

"Well, it's a damned good thing 'Ol' Jack isn't here. She 'd hear plenty of takin' the Lord's name in vain an' a whole lot more 'n that!"

It might have been the thunderstruck look on Lytle's face that got Lottie's attention. Maybe she had said too much, she suddenly caught herself, wheeled and marched back to the house. Donald went on grinding the sickle-bar, Lytle cleared his throat and made his escape to get a drink over at the watering trough and Marie went back to pedaling the grinding wheel.

"Ol' Jack" was the name which the Simms family used when they made reference to Juniper Jack Barham. Jack spent his summers up in the Blue Mountains, near Granite, Oregon, where he worked at his gold mine claim. Late in the fall of the year Jack came back to live in the bunkhouse and work as a hired man around the ranch.

Most people around the country knew him as Juniper Jack. He had had a homestead up near Paisley, but it never paid off financially. Sometimes he hired on as a hunting guide to wealthy city folks who came to hunt the Chewaucan area. His best talent was probably as a sheepherder. Lytle hired Jack to herd sheep for the Simms Ranch shortly after the war ended and gradually, over time, his home base became the bunkhouse at the Simms Ranch.

He ate his meals at Darlene's kitchen table with the rest of the family. He greatly admired Darlene and over time he developed an old man's worship of her. He respected Lottie and Lytle, worked side-by-side with Donald during lambing season, did other odd jobs about the ranch and he was, somewhat out of the ordinary for him, kindly toward Marie.

Jack had joined the Valley Falls Grange back when it was first organized. He got himself cleaned up every other Saturday night and rode down to the grange hall with the rest of the Simms family.

That summer, however, it probably was, as Donald had told his mother, a good thing that he happened to be gone from the ranch.

After Grandma Brown and Aunt Frankie went to Aunt Wilma's house in town Donald got pretty vocal about Hazel's "getting religion." Darlene didn't say anything, one way or the other, at least not in front of anyone. Lottie did finally shut him up with, "a little religion wouldn't hurt you none." Lytle, like Darlene, didn't say anything either.

At least that was the way Marie observed the situation. But at that time, she was still pretty innocent about the whole religious matter, because she had no idea what religion was even about.

Aside from all that religious fuss everyone in the Simms family considered Hazel Brown a capable and good woman.

From the time of her childhood Darlene had been taught by her mother how to do hard work. When Hazel paid her daughter the rare visit, Hazel wasn't shy about pitching in and doing even more than her share of the work. She seemed happy to do it and appeared to be somewhat relieved to "be useful." That's how she put it.

She manhandled the hoe and helped divert water through little ditches that ran through Darlene's garden. Hazel went over to Lottie's backyard and helped Lottie pick raspberries and currants. She made jams and jellies. While Darlene ran the washing machine and put laundry through the wringer over in the washhouse attached to Lottie's back porch, Hazel carried the wicker basket across the road and hung the laundry on a clothesline strung from the back of the woodshed over to the tin roof on the bunkhouse.

One Sunday morning she went out to the chicken house, grabbed the chicken hook and proceeded to snag the foot of a young spring rooster. She wrung his neck, picked the feathers, took the lid off the kitchen stove and singed it. She pulled out the innards, rinsed the cavity out good, cut it up and put the pieces to soak in clear cold water.

It was no wonder, Marie thought, that Mommy could pull off that same nasty chore just as easy as she did everything else. Marie considered her mother to be a regular wonder woman when it came to things like that and it was clear that Darlene had learned it all from Hazel Brown.

The real wonder came at dinner time when Grandma Brown and Mommy fried the chicken and made creamy chicken gravy to spoon over heaped mounds of mashed potatoes. Darlene fried up little chunks of bacon and made a dressing of thick cow's cream and vinegar to pour over young lettuce leaves picked that morning from her garden.

Aunt Frankie wasn't as keen about doing some of those things, but she had to help because Grandma told her to.

Not only that, Grandma Brown was every bit as good with the baby as Mommy was. Unlike Daddy, who was an only child, Mommy had seven brothers and sisters.

Marie watched with interest as her grandmother scooped up Raymond, changed his diaper, bathed him, fed him and jiggled him up and down until he went to sleep.

Lottie Simms, had a tendency to stand back when it came to the baby and tried not to interfere with the way Darlene did things. Hazel Brown had no such compunction; she barreled right in and did it. Not only had she raised a healthy brood of her own, she was used to her children having babies, except for Aunt Frankie who wasn't married yet. Marie had three first cousins who were born during the summer of 1943, the same summer that she was born. Grandma Brown, she thought, was kind of a wonder woman in her own way.

Marie mused while she watched Grandma Brown holding and loving Raymond. Marie wondered if her grandmother had ever held her like that. Marie supposed that she must have, but she couldn't remember it. She kind of wished that she could remember it because it must have been nice. But Marie was still shy around Grandma Brown, so she held back and Hazel didn't try to push her. Grandma Brown was a lot bigger woman than Grandmo Simms and it looked like her lap was quite ample for more than one child at a time. Hazel Brown didn't have a reluctance toward all that warm, fuzzy cuddling and hugging stuff that Lottie Simms outwardly portrayed.

"Proper" had been drilled into Lottie Chandler Simms from day-one and even though Marie had absolutely no doubt about how much her Grandmo Simms loved her, it was not often expressed in a public and outward way.

After about two weeks at the ranch, Grandma Brown and Aunt Frankie went back to town and stayed with Aunt Wilma. Aunt Wilma was her daughter, too and Iney, Aunt Wilma's daughter, was only two weeks younger than Marie.

When Grandma Brown came over from Cave Junction to visit her two Lakeview daughters, she arrived with the notion of making Iney and Marie each a new dress. She brought with her two lengths of fabulous new material that she had purchased from a fabric store in Grants Pass. The sheer, crinkly silkiness of that nylon fabric was wonderful. Iney's dress was made of the blue fabric because she had red hair and blue eyes and Marie's dress was made from the red because she had brown hair and hazel eyes. Aunt Wilma had a new electric sewing machine and so Grandma Brown set about making those dresses at Aunt Wilma's house.

The next time they were in town, Lytle dropped Darlene, Raymond and Marie off at Wilma's house for the afternoon.

Grandma Brown slipped the dress over Marie's head and pinned up the hem. She was a fast sewer and in no time the hem was finished. Then there was a flurry of picture taking.

Aunt Wilma and her husband, Troy Icenhower, ran a gas station and they lived in the back section of the building. It was in a strategic location just where the highway curved as motorists from the south entered Lakeview. It was an odd piece of property as it was in a triangular shape between a curve in the highway and a straight intersecting street. The gas station was built specifically to fit the lot.

Grandma posed Iney and Marie out front, not far from the single gas pump, and took a picture of them. Iney with her mop of curly red hair and blue eyes looked as though she was happy as a lark in her dress of sky blue. The puffed sleeves and neck were trimmed in white lace; the soft gathered skirt was fastened to a trim waist and it was tied back with a crisp bow and long streams of ribbon. Marie stood slightly pigeon-toed with her arms folded in front. Her red dress was made identical to Iney's and her straight brown hair was neatly done up in long braids that were looped and tied up with white ribbon.

The picture was in black and white so one would have to imagine the color of Iney's and Marie's dresses as they posed in front of the rather dingy service station with a bright yellow gasoline pump. The dirt road curving into the station was typically splotched here and there with ground-in oil. It was a photo of a rarely shared companionship between two first cousins who were proud as they wore dresses lovingly made by their mutual grandmother.

For as long as she could manage it, that red dress was among Marie's most prized possessions. But there came a day when Darlene could not let the hem out any further and the sleeves and waist were too tight. Darlene washed it out by hand in the kitchen sink, hung it in the shade to dry and then folded it away in the hall closet.

With added bedrooms and a connecting hallway Darlene had a hall closet similar, but somewhat less interesting, than the catchall over at Lottie's house. On the floor of that closet rested Darlene's own pile of rags and other such stuff that she wanted out of sight and out of her way. On the upper shelves of the closet, she placed items that she intended to keep in perfect condition for a long, long time, or perhaps forever. And so, the red dress was placed on a shelf with other such items of equal importance.

In the years following Bert and Hazel Brown's move from Lakeview Darlene saw very little of her mother and father. Years later Marie figured out that their parting at that move was likely the last time Darlene ever saw her father. She saw her mother sporadically after the move but it could not be considered as often. On the whole of it, Darlene's life was less needful of her parents than those of some of her brothers and sisters.

She and Donald lived good at the ranch beneath Abert Rim. Life was simple, lacking in many of the conveniences had by others, and yet Darlene, Donald and their children were loved, nurtured, protected and given all that was possible for them to give by Donald's parents, Lottie and Lytle Simms.

Years before, when she had first seen the ranch, instinct had settled within Darlene that it was a place to which she had been born and there she would spend the rest of her life. If, by even the remotest chance, her life gave her anything less than joy and full contentment it was well concealed from Darlene's fellow travelers through life.

Marie didn't think overly much on such deep interpersonal relationships, but instinct told her that that red dress held a place of importance to her mother as well as herself.

# Visitors From the East

Late that summer Donald finally broke over and bought a new car. Willys had come out with a new model and he'd been looking them over and giving some serious thought to buying one. It was just the thing they needed for traveling in and out of the ranch during winter and everyone could ride inside when they traveled up in the mountains over rough roads, which they often did. The grain crop was good and about a week before Labor Day Donald went into town and bought a brand-new forest-green Willys Jeep station wagon.

He had a trip on his mind for the coming fall. Many evenings Marie overheard her mother and father talking about it.

"I don't know why I feel the way I do, but I think we ought to go ahead this fall and make that trip down through Hells Canyon."

Darlene answered, "Your Dad's sure been talking a lot about it. If you think we should, then go ahead an' buy the station wagon. Everything you read recommends a four-wheel drive and according to the rest of what we read, they're about to go ahead with building the Hells Canyon Dam so this fall 's about our last chance."

"I figure I'll be done with the grain about a week after Labor Day. It's after school starts, but it won't hurt anything to take Marie out of school for a few days. We shouldn't be gone more 'n a week."

Darlene replied, "It's never hurt her before, and it seems like it's our best chance. Mom and Dad sure would like it. Your Dad's always ready to go somewhere."

Marie listened to this supper table conversation with barely concealed excitement. She wanted to jump up and dash over to Grandpo's and

Grandmo's house and tell them all about it. However, it was already after dark and the "fraidy cat" side of her nixed that idea.

Marie was old enough and wise enough now that she had figured out that it really wasn't her place to issue major announcements out of a clear blue sky. But on the other hand, she knew that she would always be forgiven for exciting pieces of news that were not her place to tell. Donald broke the news to Lytle and Lottie early the next morning over a cup of coffee before he went to the grain field.

No one was paying attention to any of those seemingly insignificant details, but lately it appeared that many things were going Grandpo's way. Lytle Simms was finally leading the relaxed life of a man who had worked hard, gained financial security and was surrounded by a doting family.

Lottie was washing up the breakfast dishes when two longs and one short jangled from the crank telephone that hung on the front room wall. She threw down her dishtowel and hurried through from the kitchen.

"Hello?"

"Hello. Lottie? This is Bessie. I'm sure glad I caught you inside. I thought maybe you 'd be out in the garden gatherin' up stuff for the fair booth. I just wanted to let you know that Vest had a call from Ferrin, you know, the school superintendent, an' he told Vest to drop the kids off up at the North School again. The Valley Falls kids are to go back to the North School this year."

"Oh, they are? That's a surprise."

"Yes, well Vest thought I ought to call up all the parents an' let 'em know so's they won't be surprised come Tuesday. You can tell Donald an' Darlene."

"I'll go right over and let them know."

Bessie went on, "I suppose you an' Darlene are busier 'n heck with the fair booth,"

"Yes, we're going in this afternoon to help finish it up. If I do say so myself, we've got a darned good-lookin' booth this year."

Bessie snorted out a half-laugh, "Well, you girls already know you're never gonna beat that bunch out at Thomas Creek!"

Lottie replied, "That's a fact, but we're going to give it a good try. Well, thanks, Bessie, for letting us know about the school."

And as usual and as was expected on Tuesday morning after Labor Day the majority of Lakeview school kids were somewhat sleepy eyed. The big celebration was over for another year.

As Marie climbed up the steps and took her usual seat on the bus she was pleased with her new back-to-school dress that Grandmo had splurged on over at Montgomery Ward's in Klamath Falls. She carried a brand-new red and black plaid school bag in the latest durable plastic and it was filled with fresh unopened notebooks, new scissors, a ruler and a good supply of number two pencils.

She couldn't say that she was glad, or worried, one way or the other, about going back up to the North School. She knew the teachers at both the North School and the South School now, and she also had friends at both of those schools. She was a seasoned student and it was all just something different for a new year.

Madge and Marie wanted to be in Mrs. Brosius' third-grade room. When they read the room assignments scotch-taped to the glass panes of the front door, they quickly discerned that Madge and Mike were assigned to Mrs. Brosius' class, but Marie was assigned to Mrs. Hull's room.

Oh well, Marie thought, it's just something else new and unexpected. She was used to it now. By her eighth year she was beginning to figure out that things don't always work out the way you want them to.

Both of the third-grade classes were located upstairs—in the old part of the building. It was actually a matter of pride with them, because now they were the upper classmen of the North School. A devilish instinct had been planted within them that although it was not so long ago that they were mere rank beginners they ought to take it upon themselves to emphasize to those innocent little first and second graders how wise and accomplished they had become.

During recess they liked to brag and chant: "First grade babies, second grade tots. Third grade angels, and fourth grade snots."

Mrs. Hull was delightful. She was pretty, tall, slim and very young. Brilliant morning sunshine streamed into her classroom through tall eastern windows. She adorned the room with interesting pictures, bright colored posters and geraniums in full bloom graced the window sills. Mrs. Hull smiled with eager anticipation at each of her students that first day as they filed past and took their seats.

That evening Darlene and Donald were a little surprised when Marie told them about Mrs. Hull. They surmised that they must be new people in town, because they'd never heard of them before now. They wondered what he, Mr. Hull, did. Perhaps he was a school teacher also. Well, it didn't make any difference because Marie seemed happy and they'd meet Mrs. Hull soon enough when they attended the open house in October.

Back on Friday before Labor Day weekend, Donald drove the heavily loaded grain truck up and parked it in front of the gashouse for the night. He drove in right behind Lytle who was driving everyone else out from town. Darlene and Lottie and the rest of the grange ladies had finished up the grange's fair booth around five o'clock. Those last four miles from the highway in to the ranch were hot and dusty this time of year and everyone heaved an inward sigh of relief as Lytle parked the car under the shade of those grand old Poplar trees.

"Whose car is that?" Lytle asked.

"Looks like we've got some company."

"Well, I'll be damned if that isn't a Missouri license plate!"

Questions, followed by his own answers, rolled out of Lytle's mouth.

Tom Simms leaped forward to meet his brother as Lytle opened the car door. They shook hands, slapped each other on the back and gave in to an emotional embrace. Lottie was around the car in a flash as Nellie rushed to meet her. They clasped each other as sisters who had been long apart. Although they were sisters-in-law, their bond was as strong as blood kin.

Donald jumped down from the truck and hurried over to greet his cousin, Gene, who was only a pace behind his parents.

"Why didn't you let us know? We would've been here! My goodness! What a surprise! If you aren't a sight for sore eyes!"

Darlene smiled as she held Raymond while everyone exclaimed over what a fine-looking boy he was. Marie stood back for a minute, just a little shy, but she remembered Aunt Nellie and Uncle Tom from Missouri and she liked them. She wasn't sure about Gene, though. She remembered what a terrible tease he had been when, several years ago, they had made a long, long trip back east to Missouri.

"Well sir," said Tom, "we started out to go fishin' for a few days, down at Bagnell Dam. The fishin' was dammed poor, to say the least."

"By poor, he means none," put in Gene.

Tom went on, "I told Nellie an' Gene that we should have drove out to Oregon instead of tryin' to fish, an' Gene, here, he says, 'Well hell Dad, why don't we go on anyway?' and I says we don't have enough time but Gene convinced us otherwise. So here we are!"

"How long can you stay?" asked Lottie

Nellie put in, "Oh we've got to turn right around day after tomorrow and start back. Tom's still workin' you know."

In the end it turned out that Gene convinced his father to make a long-distance call back to the lead mine where Tom worked and beg off for a few more days. He was due to retire at the end of the year and the lady in the office said, "For goodness sake, Tom, take all the time you want. You've got it comin' to you anyway."

So even though it was a very short visit for all the miles they had traveled, everyone enjoyed the visit and they all had a wonderful time.

They stayed over Saturday and Sunday and left early Monday morning before the rest of them drove into town for the Labor Day Parade.

Over Saturday everyone visited like crazy. Try as they might, it was impossible to make up for the lost years between them. Lytle took Tom all around the ranch and pointed out all the changes and the improvements that had been made since that long-ago day at the end of summer in 1929 when Tom and Nellie had had to pack up their three children, their meager belongings and return to Missouri.

The band of sheep had been sold down to around three hundred head and so there was no longer a sheepherder nor any need for camp tending chores. The ranch no longer grew potatoes, and now there were fields of grain. Most of this year's grain crop was already harvested and the fields were reduced to a prickly golden stubble. The dairy cows were gone, but Lytle had kept a couple of milk cows for their own use. Tom laughed when Lytle told him about that.

"I'll bet you don't miss milkin' all them cows now, do you Light?"

"No sireee! That's one job I can do without!"

There was a small herd of range cattle now. They couldn't see the cattle because they were scattered and grazing in the fields above the houses and the barn—up under the rim.

Lytle explained to Tom, "It's the way to go now, Tom—raisin' grain an' cattle. The market for wool is dammed near gone an' mutton an' lamb, well that never was too high on most folk's choice of what they want to eat."

Lytle chuckled as he went on, "I don't blame 'em any, 'cause myself, I'll take a good beef steak any day, over lamb."

Tom answered, "You an' Lottie are showin' good sense, Light. An' you've got Donald to carry on. Ranchin' is in his blood too an' it looks like he's raisin' a fine set of ranch hands his own self. You're doin' alright for yourselves."

"An' things have turned out good for you an' Nellie, an' your family," Lytle returned. "Lottie an' I, well we're mighty grateful for that Tom.

We were awful worried when you had to leave the ranch an' go back to Missouri. It made us plumb sick at heart that things didn't work out here. Mother an' the ol' man was terribly worried too, an' they always missed you an' the kids, but there wasn't anythin' else that could be done, at the time."

On Sunday they took two cars and drove into Lakeview to take in the fair. Lytle, Lottie, Tom, Nellie and Gene went to the rodeo. Donald and Darlene decided not to go because they knew Raymond would be a handful and even though Marie begged to go with her grandparents, Darlene said, "no."

She said, "She'll just want every hotdog and bag of popcorn that goes by. You all just need to enjoy yourselves."

Marie, of course, put on a pouty face, but for once in her life, it didn't do her any good.

That unexpected visit from the eastern part of the Simms family combined with a trip along the Snake River, at the bottom of Hells Canyon, made Lytle Simms' fall about as good as he ever wanted life to be.

Lytle buttoned up his nightshirt, while Lottie pulled a nightgown over her head and then they climbed into their tall feather bed. There were new-fangled mattresses out now and everyone raved about them but they still liked their old feather bed. Lottie let out a small sigh and Lytle turned over and laid his arm across her.

"What's got you so troubled, Kid?"

"Oh, nothing really. It's sure been a fine time this fall, hasn't it? It's been so good it almost makes me a little nervous. You know, afraid all this goodness might end."

"Yeah, it's been a real good time. Don't worry so much about things, Kid. Everything is goin' to be fine from here on out. You can just mark my word on that."

# Winter Sets In

If it had been left entirely up to him Lytle was all for buying one of those new-fangled mattresses. Lottie was the hold-out. She had a tendency to wait and see what everyone else thought about a new gadget that came on the market or for something far more decisive like buying into a whole new concept of sleeping comfort. Lytle, on the other hand, delighted in every new gadget he saw.

It was this particular trait of his that caused Lytle's and Lottie's house to be the receptacle of an interesting and eclectic variety of "stuff." Once in a while he fell for an item that did turn out to be rather useful, but there was more than one of Lytle's inability to turn a deaf ear to a convincing salesman, that was stored away in Grandmo's big closet, gathering dust on a forgotten shelf or even carried out to the loft above the horse barn.

The Modoc County Fair, down at Cedarville, California, has been held a week before the Lake County Fair for generations. Cedarville is located a tad over the California/Oregon border, about sixty miles south of Lakeview. And back in the 1950s tradition held that southern Lake County folks, in the spirit of fostering community neighborliness, drove down to Cedarville for Modoc County's big event. It wasn't unusual for a caravan of Chandler family members to make the trip: Gunthers, Ahlstroms, Newtons and Simms'.

Marie loved the fair at Cedarville. It was like a preview of coming attractions leading up to Lake County Fair and Round-Up. While she washed up and put on her fair-going outfit, Mommy or Daddy or both of them said, "Now don't be askin' for a whole bunch of stuff down there. You'd better save back for Labor Day."

Right. And wasn't Grandpo going to the fair?

They knew better, of course, but it was the expected statement issued by young parents who were doing the best they could to bring up a reasonably unspoiled child. It floated over the top of Marie's head, mainly because she knew that Grandpo was the biggest kid in the family! He'd come home with a whole bunch of stuff and very likely some of that stuff would belong to her.

There was the year of the foam rubber bed-pillow.

At the first booth inside the exhibit building a salesman was proclaiming the wonders of foam rubber pillows. Such a pillow, he said, would calm the weary soul each and every night and ease all manner of sleep discomforts. He said that once you had experienced such wonderful deep sleep, you would never again go back to a feather or down-filled pillow. Lytle Simms was the exact target he was aiming for.

That same night he was already beginning to hate that blasted pillow. No matter how many times he turned it over, tried to punch the resistant thing down, tried to scrunch it or plump it, the stubborn elastic retaining nature of that damnable foam rubber remained an unyielding rock of total discomfort. After two restless nights, due to her own lack of sleep from his tossing and turning, Lottie became cranky and rather prolific with, "I told you so's."

By the end of the week it was cast off to the bed in the other room. Aunt Lora and Uncle Harry were most often the guests who slept in that room and Uncle Harry said that he really liked the pillow. But when Grandmo offered to send it home with them they politely declined and Uncle Harry said, "Oh no you just keep it an' I'll enjoy it whenever we're out here."

Another year down at the Cedarville fair there was a salesman who showed off the very latest in furniture trends. There it was. Regally displayed on a piece of tan carpet was the most up-to-date version of a Naugahyde recliner. Never in Marie's life did she ever again see such a piece of furniture except at that fair and in Grandmo's front room.

Perhaps a more accurate description would be—lounge-chair/recliner

It had a high back, a deep dip for the seat and a long—very long—gracefully (if graceful could be applied to that particular piece of furniture) curved foot rest. The chair could be controlled with a wooden brake handle located just under the arms. It could be tipped back—way, way back—for the ultimate comfort of elevated feet. If, however, you were a couple of kids who had figured out how to have a joyride in your grandmother's front room, you could release the brake with a quick jerk for a wild ride down and up—and down and up—until it eventually came to a quivering stop. It was just right for a good-sized man (no real lady of the 1950s would have been caught dead in such an ungraceful position) or two bored kids hell-bent on having a good time.

The chair was Kelly green and had such a cumbersome shape that it took up an enormous amount of space. It had to be special ordered and shipped direct to the ranch from the factory in Indiana, or some such state back there. It was such an outlandish and expensive purchase that it even shocked Grandmo into silence. And it was substantial. It never wore out nor broke down for the rest of their mortal lives.

Lytle did feel obligated to recline in the chair every once in a while, but for the most part, grandchildren, grandnieces and grandnephews took turns forcing it backward as far as they could, pulling the brake with a quick jerk and letting it plunge and rock to a standstill. Let it be said that it was one heck-of-a-ride!

The gist of all of this is that Lytle Simms enjoyed life. His enjoyment was infectious and its glow spread over everyone in his family.

After the fun of the round-up weekend and the unexpected visit from the eastern part of the Simms family there was the wonderful trip down Hells Canyon in Donald's new jeep station wagon. Deer hunting season came and went with the usual amount of extra people hosteled at the ranch.

The Valley Falls Home Ec Club decided to run a lunch counter down at the store during hunting season to raise money for improvements on the grange hall and Darlene made huge pots of chili for that. Lottie made pies and helped run the counter. Mrs. Schofield made pies and sandwiches and waited on customers and Madge and Marie played waitress all day Saturday and Sunday.

By the time hunting season came to its end the ground was white with frost almost every morning. The brisk nip of autumn turned to rain that gathered strength and chilled into snow.

One morning Darlene rummaged for a pencil and a scrap of clean paper from the usual pile of ranch paper work piled up on the end of the kitchen counter. She sat down at the table and began to make out a list of what she needed from the store for Thanksgiving. Across the table Donald tipped his head back and swallowed the last dregs from his mug.

"I'm sure as hell glad we went ahead an' bought that little caterpillar. I got a feeling that that dozer blade's gonna come in damned handy this winter."

Darlene got up and lifted Raymond from his high chair as she answered, "It's probably a good thing, alright. It feels like winter's here to stay already."

Donald continued to gloat, "An' all that winter wheat in the ground—this is perfect weather for it. Well, let ol' man winter come. We're as ready as we've ever been, an' more so at that."

As an eight-year-old child Marie did not have a reference point from which she could measure the contentment and security she innocently took for granted. She jammed her arms into her winter coat and ran out to the jeep where Daddy already had the heater going. Her immediate problem was getting to the school bus on time.

Thursday was Thanksgiving. There would be a huge roasted turkey that Grandpo had raised. There would be mounds of stuffing, and piles of mashed potatoes and gravy, and Grandmo's homemade potato rolls and mincemeat pie, and Aunt Gladys' steamed carrot pudding topped with a piece of hard sauce melting down into all that gooey softness, and all the aunts and uncles and cousins would be there.

Only two weeks after Thanksgiving it would be her baby brother's first birthday. Then Daddy would bring in two Christmas trees. She would help Mommy as they decorated one of the trees in their own front room and the other tree would be for Grandmo's and Grandpo's house.

Loggers would bring a giant tree from the forest and men from the sawmill would help secure it in the intersection between the courthouse and the bank. Marie's class was busy practicing the Christmas songs they would sing on the night of the Elk's Christmas tree when everyone gathered around that magnificent tree uptown. Grandpo was a member of the Elks lodge and so he would help pass out bags filled with Christmas candy, nuts and oranges. They made sure that every child in Lakeview got one of those bags.

Not only was there all of that goodness, but on the last Sunday afternoon before Christmas, there would be a dinner and a Christmas program down at the Grange Hall. She and Madge and the Counts boys and all the other kids that were coming out from town to the grange now, were busy practicing songs and skits for that. There would be a big Christmas tree in the grange hall—just in front of that big chalk mural of Abert Rim. They'd leave the grange hall tree up until after the New Year's Eve party.

There was so much hustle and bustle from one event to the other that no one had time to pay much attention to the snow that was piling up. Except for Donald. He noticed, and he was darned grateful for that little D3 dozer. He plowed out the road day after day. The track into the ranch went deeper and deeper into a canyon of dirty white banks packed full of ice and snow.

They all had Christmas dinner in town at Aunt Gladys' house that year, because it was hard to get in to the ranch.

School took up after Christmas break and everyone settled in for the duration.

One night, Darlene heard restless tossing and turning along with an occasional moan coming from Marie's room. And there it came! Darlene threw the covers back and rushed down the hall. She wasn't fast enough, of course, and Donald sank back in bed cussing, but not loud enough to wake the baby. He listened while Darlene cleaned up the soiled mess and tossed the smelly laundry out on the back porch. Maybe there is something to gettin' one of them new automatic washin' machines, he thought.

Darlene comforted Marie, felt her forehead, and yes indeed, she has a fever. She removed Marie's soiled nightgown and saw the telltale red spots.

The next morning Lottie got out her doctor book and read up on how to treat measles. Darlene called up Dr. Wilbur and asked what he thought about Raymond's being exposed. Dr. Wilbur assured her that the baby would most likely have a very mild case and said, "Just let it go ahead an' happen. He'll be fine."

Once the pukey stage was over the measles turned into a long boring, disgusting time. The room had to be kept dark. Marie couldn't even read one of her new Christmas gift Bobbsey Twins books. Daddy barely peeked his head around her bedroom door because he wasn't fond of seeing her pimply red polka dotted complexion. Daddy didn't have a strong constitution when it came to being around other people's ailments. That tendency was showing up more and more as he progressed into parenthood.

One nice thing was that Marie could have all the tomato and orange juice she wanted to drink. Grandmo and Grandpo made a trip into town and Grandmo stopped by the Mercantile and bought more of those tall cans of juice. You had to be sick before you could have all the juice you wanted. That's how they still rationed out those kinds of things at the ranch. Then Mommy made eggnog t0 build up her strength. Mommy's eggnog was almost worth the whole bother of being sick.

Grandmo said that she almost bought a pair of red polka dot pajamas for Marie and Marie was intensely glad that she settled on a pair that had a print of root-beer barrel candy instead.

During the first week of February Lytle went in to town by himself one day. Before he left town, he felt that he could sense a bad storm coming on. It wasn't quite time for school to be out, but he stopped by the school anyway and picked up Marie. Mrs. Hull quickly gathered up homework assignments to send home with her and it was a good thing because the storm turned out to be a regular four days blizzard. After the storm blew itself out it took a few more days for Donald to dig everything out and get the road plowed. He only had to plow down to the end of the lane because the county snowplow came in that far. So far it had been a long, hard winter and he was sure grateful for that.

Early one morning he huddled over the cook stove for a few minutes before he poured himself another cup of coffee, pulled out a chair and sat down.

"No lambs yet this morning?" Darlene asked.

"No. I hope to hell they hold off for a while. Everything's froze harder 'n a rock. Well, at least we can get out. It's the middle of February though an' we can expect lambs most anytime now."

"Your Dad's sure not been feeling good lately."

"Yeah, seems like he's livin' on Alka Seltzer and those Currier tablets he swears by. You're goin' in to town with them today, aren't you?"

"Yes. I'd better stock up and I'll pick up some nipples for bummer lambs while I'm at it. Your Dad oughta go up to the doctor but I don't suppose he'll do it."

"No. No there's no chance of that happening. He says he doesn't like havin' to sit around the waiting room with pregnant women and sick kids."

Darlene nodded her head, "Well there's nothing we can do about it."

# What She Learned

It was out of kilter from the beginning.

Mommy gently took hold of her shoulder. "It's time to get up, Marie. Hurry and get your clothes on. We're running late this morning."

Mommy was already dressed in her going-to-town clothes. Marie rubbed the sleep from her eyes, struggled out of bed and tried her best to hurry as she hastened into clothes that Mommy was pulling from dresser drawers and yanking from the closet. The usual cold of February had a new kind of urgency this morning.

Out in the kitchen Raymond sat in his high chair. He too was cleaned up and dressed for going to town. He was getting so big now that Darlene seldom used the diaper bag for him anymore but there it was, on top of the dryer, sides bulging with extra clothes and a few toys poked out from the open top.

She sat down and looked at her bowl of mush. She tried to pick up her spoon and eat, but this morning the oatmeal looked like a bowl of colorless lumpy goop. She heard the door slam shut out on the backporch as ol' Jack stamped snow from his boots.

On short winter school days she often didn't see ol' Jack until suppertime. He and Grandpo would be letting the sheep out of the barn right now. Ol' Jack and Daddy and Grandpo ate their breakfast late—after the livestock was taken care of.

Just as ol' Jack opened the kitchen door, Donald walked out of the bathroom; he was shaved and dressed for town also.

"Eat, Marie. Let's hurry along now." Mommy prodded.

No one said anything as Daddy walked over and went down on his haunches beside Marie. He laid his hand on her leg and gave it a firm little pat as he said, "Sister, I'm sorry to have to tell you this, but Grandpo is pretty sick."

"Grandpo?"

"Yes. The Disaster Car came last night an' took Grandpo to the hospital. Grandmo went with him an' now we're goin' in too. Mommy an' I. Now everything's gonna be alright. We're gonna leave you off at the bus an' you go on to school—just the same as always. Be a good girl now, hurry up an' eat your breakfast. Do what Mommy says."

She looked up at Mommy. Mommy leaned down and silently kissed her on the top of her head.

Donald stood up and said to no one in general, "Damned good thing I got that road plowed out yesterday."

Then he turned to 'ol Jack and began to tell him about what he ought to do with the sheep and the milk cows and everything else around the ranch that needed tended to each and every day. Everything was a blur of rushing about and instructions.

Grandpo sick? And Grandmo was at the hospital with him? How could all that happen in the middle of the night and she didn't know?

The disaster car came and she didn't hear?

Marie was too young to understand that a contented and peaceful child can sleep through anything. To her, it felt as though she must have left planet earth some time during the night and now she was ever so slowly falling back to her place at the kitchen table.

"Let's go now, Marie. Everything's gonna be alright."

If Daddy said so, then it must be right, she thought. Daddy wouldn't tell me anything unless he thought it was going to be that way.

And Grandmo—she's with Grandpo. She won't let anything happen to him. Grandmo knows how to do everything.

Down at the store she got out of the car and climbed on the bus. The bus had been running for a while because Vest had already been down to the Clark ranch, at the south end of Abert Lake, and picked up the Overton boy so the bus was already nice and warm.

Just like he did yesterday Vest drove the bus to town, she went to class, and at noon she had lunch in the cafeteria.

After lunch everyone settled into the afternoon and it hardly registered on Marie's mind when the sound of Mrs. Laura Barry's click-clacking high heels accompanied by the jangling and tinkling of her jewelry came up the stairway and down the hall. She opened the door to Mrs. Hull's class and in her usual bellow she announced that "Marie Simms has been asked to walk to her Aunt May Ahlstrom's house."

For Mrs. Hull's benefit she added, "Make sure she's bundled up good in her coat and her boots."

Mrs. Hull hustled Marie into the cloak room, took her coat from the hook and helped her sort through the pile of dripping boots. Through it all, young Mrs. Hull was her sweet, lovely and kind self but it did little to reassure Marie.

Walk to Aunt May's house?

Inside of her head there was a silent scream. I don't know how to do such a thing! I don't even know the way! Or do I? I've never had to do anything like this before.

She was almost defeated by the thought of this unthinkable task that she was suddenly told to accomplish. And accomplish it, she must. She had, of course, ridden to Aunt May's house in the car many times. She knew perfectly well where Aunt May's house was located and apparently Mommy and Daddy knew that she knew too.

But all by herself?

This must be very important, she thought, and with her mind whirling and twirling and her back ramrod straight she marched out the front door, down the steps, turned onto the sidewalk and began her walk.

She crossed the intersection and walked past Graham's Chevrolet and continued on past the gas station on the corner. She walked past the parking lot beside Safeway, crossed the street and just beyond the Mercantile she turned left and walked east by Snyder and Howard's drug store, the News and Sweets and on the corner by the Mary Jo Shop she crossed and turned south by the Courthouse block. She continued on past the concrete bandstand and crossed the intersection beyond the courthouse.

Her confidence increased because now she was sure that she was on Aunt May's and Uncle Elmer's street—E Street. She didn't know that it was called E Street on that cold February day of 1952. She just knew that it was the right street.

Houses grew more and more familiar. She expelled her breath in a slight puff of cold air as she opened the gate, dashed up the path and walked into Aunt May's front room just as if it was any other ordinary day.

It was years later when she figured out what it was that propelled her beyond her own strength and guided her through the cold snowy streets of Lakeview from the North School to Aunt May's house down on South E Street. Even on that scary day she realized that it didn't feel like her own body and her own will. Her rubber galoshes strode one in front of the other, turned at all the right corners and like a magic trick that she didn't understand, there she was, in Aunt May's front room.

A quiet sort of confusion swarmed through the house. Mommy helped her out of her coat and took her galoshes to drip on the linoleum in the front entry way. Aunt Lora and Uncle Harry were there, too. Aunt Gladys stuck her head in the front door to announce that she was going back to work and that just as soon as she and Kelt were off they'd come back.

Aunt May looked a bit hurried. She still wore her bib apron from cooking something or other as she hung up the wall phone and explained, "That was Ottie. She ran home for lunch so's she could call to let us know that everything's about the same."

On that day, and for years to come, the family felt that sometimes it was a rather fortuitous stroke of luck that both Aunt Ottie Chandler and Aunt Pauline Chandler worked down at the hospital. After Aunt Ottie and Uncle George sold the Station ranch they moved to a house in town that was located just across a vacant lot from the hospital. Right away Aunt Ottie went to work in the hospital laundry.

Lottie sniffed a bit as she declared, "Well she might as well do the hospital's laundry, as well as her own."

Ottie Chandler was well justified in her reputation as an immaculate housekeeper to an extreme degree. Her sisters-in-law and her neighbors excused Ottie's ultra-cleanliness as being the result of never having been blessed with children underfoot, thus giving her the advantage in that department over the rest of them.

Lottie, herself, was inclined to get out the field glasses every New Year's Day as she scanned the situation over at the Station to see if Ottie had her sheets hanging on the clothesline. Lytle laughed at Lottie and teased her about being a nosey busybody. She answered right back with, "You know they say that whatever you do on New Year's Day, you'll do all year."

Maybe they really meant, "For the rest of your life" because that's exactly what happened to Aunt Ottie Chandler.

Back in the early 1940s Pauline and Roy Chandler moved into town from their ranch out in Crooked Creek. Not long after that Roy died from tick fever. Pauline had a talent for nursing. She had certainly done plenty of if, in her life so far, for her family and neighbors and so it was no surprise to anyone when she went to work for the hospital as a nurse's aide. For the rest of her working life Aunt Pauline Chandler walked two blocks from her house over to the hospital.

Aunt May's house felt claustrophobic that afternoon.

Marie wasn't sure that she wanted to know, but Mommy told her anyway that Grandpo wasn't getting any better and that Grandmo thought he might rally some if he could see her and Raymond, so Daddy was coming to take them down to the hospital. The thought of going to the hospital and seeing Grandpo so sick scared her, but for once in her short life she kept her thoughts to herself.

Raymond woke up and Darlene carried him from the back bedroom and put him down on the carpet beside a small pile of toy cars that Aunt May had brought out. Marie recognized the cars from when their cousin Billy Alberger had been there last summer. Billy was Aunt May's grandson who lived up in Portland.

Raymond made motor sounds as he pushed the cars around while Marie sat cross-legged beside him thumbing through a pile of magazines.

Aunt May and Grandmo both had piles of interesting magazines. They were full of beautiful ladies dressed in stylish clothes and pictures of rooms decorated in the latest trendy style. Marie had started to notice that there was a vast difference between those stylish living rooms, kitchens and bedrooms and the look of their houses out at the ranch. Whenever she thumbed through those magazines, she began to think that she wouldn't mind living in houses like those someday, but this afternoon none of those imaginations held much allure for her.

An hour went by and Daddy didn't show up. Another hour and another hour went by and it began to grow dark outside. Aunt Gladys and Uncle Kelt came in from work; everyone milled restlessly about; the smell of food permeated from the kitchen and other people, neighbors and friends, came in and out, some of them bringing dishes of food. Darlene checked on Raymond and smiled politely as she answered questions from various people. A leaden feeling hung over it all.

Marie looked up as, once again, the front door opened. Raymond squealed with delight and ran to the door because finally it was Daddy. Although the long afternoon was over, she almost dreaded to see him because she didn't know what was expected of her. He put his arm around

Mommy and said something too low for Marie to hear and then he walked over with Raymond in his arms and sat on the couch beside Marie. Mommy sat beside Daddy. She fussed at Raymond a little, pulled his pants leg down and reached over to brush loose tendrils of hair from Marie's forehead.

Daddy said, "I don't think it's a good idea to take you to the hospital. I'm afraid Grandpo's awful sick. I'm going back to the hospital now and I want you to wait here with Mommy. Be good kids an' don't mess things up for your Aunt May."

He stood up, put Raymond in Darlene's arms, laid his hand on Marie's shoulder and gave her a slight squeeze before he turned and disappeared again through the front door. That was all. It seemed like he came and went in a whirlwind, but that one squeeze on her shoulder meant that he expected her to act like a big girl, help Mommy as much as she could and be a lot braver than she felt like being.

After a while it was bedtime. Aunt Gladys and Uncle Kelt and Aunt Lora and Uncle Harry went home. Uncle Elmer took Raymond to the back bedroom where Aunt May still had a crib and he turned down the bed for Darlene and Donald.

Aunt May's front bedroom had a set of twin beds and Aunt May fussed as she rummaged in her closets for an extra blanket or two while Mommy helped Marie undress down to her slip. She said that she could sleep like that for this one night. She pulled the blankets around Marie and followed Aunt May out. She pulled the door almost shut—but not quite. A sliver of light from the front room still showed through.

The light stayed on and Marie wasn't sure but she felt like Mommy and Aunt May and Uncle Elmer sat in the front room waiting. Waiting for Daddy she guessed, she didn't know exactly what they were waiting for. She drifted off to sleep hearing their voices, very low, as someone said something every now and then.

Sometime in the night the light grew wider as Grandmo came through the door and sat down on the edge of Marie's bed. Very soft and ever so tender she laid her hand on Marie's forehead and stroked her fingers down her cheek as she whispered, "Grandpo said for me to always take good care of you. You and I will have to be best pals from now on."

Marie laid there as still as she could; she was too scared to move or even take a breath. Finally, Grandmo stood up and walked over to the other bed and sat down on the side. She just sat there—not moving and hardly breathing, herself.

Marie squeezed her eyes shut, as tight as she could. She was too old to cry. She was too bewildered to say anything to her grandmother. She sensed that Grandmo still sat on the edge of the other bed, that her elbows were propped on her knees with her head bowed low in her hands.

Lottie Chandler Simms was numb, she could not feel a thing and still she was chilled to the bone. More so than her granddaughter could possibly imagine. Marie's life was still so young and until this night, her soul was yet to be tried.

Somewhere down, down, way deep inside her body and her soul—deeper than she thought she could ever go—Marie was angry. She wasn't sure why, but she knew that she was mad at something and she didn't even know who or what it was that she was mad at. Her instinct told that someday she would have to get over it and that she was expected do her best to act like a proper young lady by the time that the sun poked up its unfailing head tomorrow morning.

But for this time, in the dark of the night with a sliver of light shining through the crack in the door, she was mad.

# A New Normal

Funeral days began the next morning. A numbness hung in the atmosphere inside Aunt May's and Uncle Elmer's house and at the same time the need for hustle and bustle and getting things done prevailed. The Chandler family backup system took over.

Marie never knew if it went as an unspoken acknowledgement, but the refuge of Aunt May's house softened the sting of that unthinkable blow in the middle of last night. For Donald and his family, her house was the glimpse of a far-away port in a storm. For Lottie, the comfort of her sister's home was salvation.

Aunt Gladys and Uncle Kelt lived in a funny house across the street from Aunt May. When their house had burnt down late in the 1940s, and they began to rebuild they started by building a basement. Word in the family was that Aunt Gladys' taste ran ahead of their bank account and so they were forced to stop with the basement until their bank account caught up. In 1952 their bank account was still in a holding pattern. They had partitioned the basement into a two-bedroom apartment and when it was furnished with Aunt Gladys' stylish taste in furniture and fixtures the inside became a comfortable home. Viewed from the street it looked rather odd, but on the inside, it was quite tasteful.

Aunt Lora and Uncle Harry lived in a meager house down in the south-end of town, but they were at Aunt May's every day, all day long, in support of Lottie for the duration of those funeral days.

Uncle Harry maintained his and Aunt Lora's huge front yard in a style fit for the cover of a home and garden magazine. Their house, however, was set far back from the street and in total contrast to the front yard the house was tiny. In truth of the matter, it was little more than a well-insulated and a well-plumbed shack. In Aunt Lora's case, word in the family had it that Uncle Harry, although a plumber with a reputation for impeccable work, spent too much time and money drinking and gambling up at the Elks Lodge.

It wasn't until Marie was a grown woman that she began to figure out that all of that "word in the family" business might appear to be gossip, or back-biting, but apparently when it happens among blood sisters it is considered a forgiven sin. Lottie and Lytle had the ranch of course, and Aunt May's life, at least on the outside, appeared to be like a beautiful placid lake.

That is the briefest of descriptions for the lifestyles of the four Chandler sisters, but different as they were, no matter what came their way, good or bad, the four sisters faced the world with a united and steel front.

Aunt Ottie Chandler and Aunt Pauline Chandler, Lottie's sisters-in-law weren't there very much. They had both been widowed from the two Chandler brothers not long ago, and even though she didn't think much about it at the time, later Marie supposed their absence was because of the rawness of their own widowhood—especially Aunt Ottie who had no children. The sisters, including Lottie, appeared to forgive them, especially Aunt Ottie, because she was—well—just different.

For Marie, her anger of the previous night turned into a blur of time and people. They all came and they all went: friends, family and neighbors. She had been taught manners and so she sat where she was told to sit, ate when, where and what she was told to eat. She went to other people's houses, even when she didn't want to go, so that she could be entertained by cousins her own age.

Down inside, however, she began to simmer all over again because it seemed like all the grown-ups were having a grand time. There was a ton of Christmas and Thanksgiving kinds of food on the table and then someone or the other would start telling funny stories about Grandpo and everyone had a good laugh.

Somewhere in that blur of time they made a trip out to the ranch. They gathered up dress clothes for the funeral while Daddy checked on everything. The neighbors were pitching in to help ol' Jack with the feeding. Daddy said that he "hoped to hell the sheep held off lambing for a few more days." Loyd Chandler was at the ranch every day and Vest and Bessie Carroll said they'd make sure that ol' Jack got in to the funeral.

During the drive out the subject of Marie's maturity as it pertained to death came up. She sat in the car's back seat where Grandpo would usually be sitting with her between him and Grandmo. Raymond was in his usual riding-in-the-car place which was standing between Mommy and Daddy on the front seat. Once in a while he turned around and looked over the back of the seat at Grandmo and Marie.

Darlene said, "I think he wonders where Dad is."

Donald said, "What about Marie? Do you think she ought to go to the funeral?"

The question wasn't really directed to Lottie, but she put in anyway, "She needs to go. She's plenty old enough and it'll be the last chance she has to see her grandfather."

Mommy didn't say what she thought, one way or the other, but after a short silence she said, "She can wear that little blue skirt you got her for Valentine's. She got a chocolate smear on it but I got the stain out and it's as good as new."

Lottie continued, "I suppose it's just as well that Ottie says she won't go and that way she can keep Raymond down at her house. Well, that's her excuse." She let out a sigh and then straightened up her shoulders.

For once in her life Marie understood that "children should be seen and not heard."

Darlene went up to the attic, dug out and dusted off a couple of suitcases and then she helped Marie find her skirt. She laid out her white ruffled blouse, the one with puffed sleeves, and instructed her to get out some clean white anklets to wear with her dress-up shoes. Marie liked that pretty skirt because it had a ruffle on the bottom and a wide sash was tied into a bow at the back. Little did she know that she could never bring herself to wear it again, and Mommy didn't insist about it either.

The weather held off for the funeral, staying clear and cold. Everyone said how glad they were about that.

Because Lytle was a member of the Elks, Lottie decided to have his funeral in the grand lodge room up on the third floor of the Elks building. Engraved in big letters near the top on the outside it says, "Heryford Building – 1913," but in the 1950s it was owned by the Elks and everyone called it the "Elks Building." The main entrance was through double doors on the south side, across Center Street from the court house. On the right side of the tiled entrance, stairs led upward and back then a set of double glass doors on the left opened into The Mercantile. An elevator that was enclosed in a black iron cage was located beside the stairway, but it was too narrow for a casket.

The family was seated behind a folding screen that zigzagged across the back side of the dark mahogany casket. The air in the room was heavy with a damp aroma drifting off the bank of floral arrangements.

Donald parked Lottie's and Lytle's good car right beside the hearse and as they got out of the car Darlene took hold of Marie's hand so that she could guide her up the stairs, to their seats and where ever it was that she was supposed to be and whatever it was that she was supposed to do.

Looking back, Marie remembered that Mommy never once let go of her hand from the minute they got out of the car.

Aunt Lora, knowing about all things that pertained to the latest in music, had said that there was a new gospel song out that was gaining popularity and so someone sang it: "It is no secret what God can do. What He's done for others, He'll do for you." Marie didn't entirely understand the song, but it sounded nice. When it was over, there was a long wait behind that screen while the crowd filed past the casket and finally it came time for the family.

Mommy led her around the screen so that she could look at Grandpo. Mommy only paused for a second before she whisked Marie away and they began to walk down those long, long stairs into the crowd standing about on the muddy white tiles of the entrance. The crowd spilled out the open doors and up and down the street. Some of them briefly touched her as Mommy guided her through; they talked in low voices and some of them said what a big funeral it was.

Marie was dazed. She looked dazed and she acted dazed. Looking down at her, Darlene said, "Do you want to go down and stay at Ottie's while we go to the cemetery?"

"Yes, Mommy."

"Hurry, then. I can make it down there and back while they bring Dad down. It's going to take a few minutes."

Mommy clutched her hand while they ran through the crowd and across the highway between The Mercantile and the Hardware store. They ran past the Catholic Church, crossed the street by the hospital, ran down beside the vacant lot behind the hospital and across H Street to Aunt Ottie's house. It was slippery, but they clenched their toes and hung on—Marie in her black patent Mary Jane's and Darlene in her ivory high-heels trimmed with brown wing tips. They ran up Aunt Ottie's back steps and into the open arms of her warm house. Raymond sat on the rug in front of her dining room stove. He was quiet and still for once in his life, mesmerized by the trill of her song birds.

The first time that Marie saw that plot of ground out at the cemetery, where they had left Grandpo, it was warm and the ground was bare of the winter's ice and snow.

The next morning, they went back out to the ranch.

Donald drove the car into the garage and they carried stuff from the car through Lottie's side door that opened off of her dinette. ol' Jack and Loyd were still out tending the sheep and hadn't had time to light a fire so the house was cold. Donald started a fire in the front room while Darlene lit a fire in the kitchen. Everyone but Donald huddled around the stoves for a few minutes. He turned and said that he was going on out to the barn.

Darlene answered, "Alright. I'll help Mom get things put away."

They didn't go on across the road to their own house that night, Darlene, Donald, Marie and Raymond; instead they huddled up in Lottie's house. Darlene cooked supper and ol' Jack said that he was plenty glad to plow through the snow drifts from the bunkhouse clear over to Lottie's for someone else's cookin'.

Donald and Darlene took Raymond in with them as they slept in Lottie's spare bedroom.

Marie slept in Grandmo's bed, in the place where Grandpo used to sleep.

She went back to school the next morning.

They kept putting off going on over to their own house while the weather was still so bitter and cold. The sheep began to lamb and they got through that first lambing season without Lytle. When it came time, Loyd Chandler came up just like he always did to help Donald and ol' Jack dock and earmark the lambs.

One day Darlene moved the stuff that had made its way over to Lottie's back over to their house. She gave the downstairs a good spring cleaning, cleaned out and straightened up the refrigerator and generally put their lives back to order. That night she cooked supper in her own kitchen and asked Lottie to come over and eat with them.

Donald and Darlene slept in their own bed that night and Raymond in his crib, but after supper Marie went back over to Grandmo's house. She couldn't bear to think of her being alone and Mommy and Daddy said that it was okay for another night. And then there was another night and the night after that and it kept on and on.

Sometimes in the middle of the night, when Grandmo thought she was sound asleep, Marie would hear her talking to Grandpo. She would whisper, "Lytle, Lytle." Grandmo never cried, but nevertheless her smothered sorrow broke Marie's heart.

She couldn't say so to Mommy and Daddy, but when Marie would try to sleep in her own bed, in her own room, she was not able to get those forlorn whispers out of her mind. Then she called out, "Mommy, I have to go back to Grandmo's."

In their room, just down the hall, Donald mumbled something to Darlene, and then Darlene threw back the covers and said, "I'll turn on the yard light and help you get across."

# Lessons of Spring

A new pace of life settled over the Simms Ranch as Marie went back to school. After Lytle Simms' death she was a little wiser, but on the other hand, not so much either. With Grandpo's passing her eyes had been opened to the heartbreak of human death.

She was used to the death of ranch animals; it was a fact of ranch life that caused them to be rather insensitive in that regard. During lambing season, death was something that she witnessed every day.

When the lambs were dropping, the regular mound of manure and rotting barn scrapings that Donald semi-annually pushed out with the tractor blade was topped by another layer made up of dead lambs. Donald and ol' Jack added more carcasses to the pile every morning. When Donald found a little extra time (he gauged it sometime before nighttime temperatures rose above freezing and sometime before daytime temperatures warmed) he threw the frozen carcasses into the pickup bed and hauled them to a site well away from the ranch buildings. Far enough so that the eventual smell of decay wouldn't drift back to the houses. He poured a bottle of strychnine over the heap and thus any cayotes who visited the site would also be killed.

Cows, calves and adult sheep died and every-once-in-a-while a beloved horse would "pass beyond the great divide." That's how Grandmo put it.

Up until Grandpo's passing, the eternal loss of someone she loved had never been tried in Marie's life. When Grandpa Brown passed away, all she remembered was traveling to his funeral—she did not remember being a part of his living existence. Grandpa Brown's passing did not cause any kind of alteration to her life. Marie did remember "old Grandpo," who was Lytle's own father, Will Simms, but because old

Grandpo's death occurred so early in her life it had slipped by quietly and almost unnoticed.

Marie liked to help Grandpo take dinner into the old man's room. At meal time, her grandmother would place old Grandpo's plate and his cup of coffee onto a cutting board that she had pulled out from underneath the kitchen counter. Her grandfather carried the board to the old man's room and placed it across the wide wooden arms of his chair. Marie considered herself quite helpful as she skipped ahead to open the door to old Grandpo's room.

One day she suddenly noticed that old Grandpo's room was empty and he was not to be found anywhere. When she asked where old Grandpo had disappeared to, she was given a noncommittal answer and because she was so young and had no real emotional attachment to the old man, she accepted the answer with no further thought.

That spring after old Grandpo's disappearance Donald and Lytle began remove the wall that separated the old man's room from the rest of Lottie's and Lytle's house as they made an addition for their front room. As they remodeled, they placed a grand set of windows in the southern wall. Those windows were made up of small individual panes that stretched across the entire wall. When the room was done and Lottie finished hanging her new curtains, southern light streamed through those glistening panes and everyone stood back and admired the panoramic view over the southern end of the valley.

Spring of 1952 began its usual tiptoeing kind of arrival at the ranch beneath Abert Rim. It would burst in one day only to retreat for another week and then start its arrival all over again. During that spring when Marie went back to school after her grandfather's funeral, she began to realize that she had gained some knowledge about life and death that she would have rather not known. She often found herself pondering over this new piece of unwelcome information.

Mrs. Hull, her third-grade teacher, was an earnest and devout Christian woman. Mrs. Hull, however, was still somewhat innocent and that no doubt was due to her own youth. Because there was no rule against it in the public-school system back then, each day she read bible passages to her classroom. Up until Mrs. Hull's entrance into her life, Marie's knowledge of the bible was almost nonexistent except for when Grandma Brown visited and prayed over meals, or when prayers were offered by Mrs. Schofield or Minnie Counts over meals down at the grange hall. That spring, as the Easter season approached, Mrs. Hull's bible stories suddenly began to enlarge Marie's biblical knowledge almost to the point of complete horror.

Marie had a good understanding of the fact that Jesus was a baby born in a manger long, long ago in a place far, far away. That was Christmas. There were donkeys and cows and sheep and shepherds (not sheepherders like 'ol Jack, but nicely cleaned up shepherds) standing about him and gazing in rapt adoration.

Because her knowledge was so limited, Marie had a hard time relating that Baby Jesus to the grownup man who loved all little children as well as everything and everyone else in the whole wide world. Until that spring and Mrs. Hull's bible passages relating the Easter story, she had been spared the knowledge of his crucifixion.

Crucifixion, she discovered to her horror, was another word for intentional murder. Jesus, once a beautiful baby in a manger, was murdered at the hands of other human beings. Intentionally and methodically killed in such a cruel and horrific way that she could not even bear to hear it! She didn't want to hear any more bible stories because they drove her into night time terrors.

"Maybe Daddy's right," she said to herself.

Whenever the subject of religion came up, which wasn't very often, or once in a while when there was a movie about something that happened in biblical times that came to the Marius Theater or the Alger Theater in town, and Grandmo and Mommy wanted to go see it, Daddy would grumble and mutter and maintain that he didn't want to hear or see anything about "Moses in the bulrushes." But then he would wind up doing it anyway to please Mommy and Grandmo.

However, all of that soulful pondering about biblical terror and sadness over life and death did not seem to dampen her enthusiasm for the coming Easter. There was a good reason. She looked forward to receiving an Easter basket that was bound to be chock full of odds and ends of little girl trinkets, a new outfit that Grandmo was sure to buy and she was especially fond of those beautiful chocolate eggs and chocolate bunnies that came from the dime store in town.

Virginia Crummett, who was one of Donald's cousins (her maiden name being Chandler) had grown up on the Heat Chandler ranch down on Crooked Creek. Virginia, having been the person who introduced Donald and Darlene to each other back in 1942, was also one of Mommy's best friends. Virginia, now married to Floyd Crummett, lived in Lakeview and she worked uptown at McCaw's dime store.

For about a week to ten days leading up to Valentine's Day and Easter Sunday Virginia sat at a card table positioned in the dime store window while she decorated chocolate candies. Passersby often stopped to view her work. She decorated hollow chocolate hearts and cupids for Valentine's Day, and for Easter she decorated chocolate bunnies and chocolate eggs. Folks liked to watch as she applied frosting from plastic tubes in careful strokes creating colorful swirls, curlicues, flowers and leaves. With a final flourish she personalized each of her creations with someone's name. Children hoped against hope that their mother, or grandmother or aunt or some such person had ordered one of those marvelous chocolate creations for them!

In Marie's opinion they were too beautiful to eat and she didn't care all that much for candy, anyway, so Grandmo let her store them on the bottom shelf of her refrigerator. Grandmo's refrigerator wasn't crammed full of stuff like Mommy's was, and Grandmo was more inclined to be understanding about things like that. On average, it took about two years for Lottie to get sick and tired of chocolate bunnies, eggs and hearts filling up her refrigerator and then a grand cleaning-out took place.

That same year, after spring vacation, Mrs. Hull had another energetic idea and she began to talk to her classroom about the idea of putting on a circus.

They would entertain the other students up at the North School plus teachers and parents. Everyone grew quite excited, but Marie had a built-in country girl's apprehension about the whole matter. What could she do for such a performance? Town kids could partner up and perfect their acts in the evenings at each other's houses. Various groups signed up to be acrobats, magicians, monkeys, tigers and elephants while helpful mothers applied their own talent at sewing machines as they made costumes and directed practice sessions.

Mrs. Hull had a plan for Marie and straightaway she sent a note home to Darlene Simms. As soon as Mommy read the note, she went over to Grandmo's house and together they began to work on Marie's participation in the now highly-anticipated coming attraction of Mrs. Hull's third grade classroom circus.

Marie was to be the ticket lady.

Mrs. Hull wanted Marie to be dressed as outrageous and glamorous as Darlene would allow. She would be seated at a table outside the classroom door where upon collecting the required admission she would present a ticket to each circus spectator.

Darlene Simms went into full compliance mode.

Lottie Simms devoted an entire top shelf of the wardrobe built into the hallway between her two bedrooms to hats. Lots and lots of hats. The hats did tend to be on the demure side of fashion, somewhat like Lottie Simms herself. However, they were the kinds of hats that current stylish ladies of Lakeview, Oregon were wearing in 1952 and Lottie never passed up the opportunity to buy a new hat whenever she made a trip over to Klamath Falls.

Lottie and Darlene found a velvet hat that was draped with a smidgeon more than a discreet amount of veil. Three small brown feathers were attached somewhat off-center, just a bit to the right. Lavender gloves that Grandmo wore on her tiny hands were found and they were only slightly too large for Marie's now almost nine-year-old hands.

Lottie also kept an upholstered shoe box. Her feet were so small that Marie and her cousin, Sharon, loved to dig in that shoe box and wear Grandmo's shoes on their own fast-growing feet. At the very bottom of the shoe box was a pair of pink satin evening slippers, just sloppy enough to add outrageous appeal to Marie's costume.

Darlene bought some Paisley print material at the J.C. Penny Store in town and she sewed a long, gathered skirt. The skirt was paired with a brand-new store-bought silky white blouse. Long strings of beads and sparkly gold and silver brooches from Grandmo's jewel box finished the ensemble.

On the day of the circus Mommy came early to help Marie dress and apply lipstick, rouge and powder. Everyone exclaimed over how beautiful and glamorous she was and she never forgot how very fine and special she felt that day.

In order to squeeze all of the planned attendees into the classroom they held one performance in the morning and another in the afternoon. As spectators filed into the room, Marie collected the admission price of one button. When the circus was over, she presented Mrs. Hull with her basket-full of buttons in various and mysterious sizes, shapes, colors and designs.

Mrs. Hull had kept a secret plan for those buttons. She made them into a long rope as she strung the buttons, one at a time, onto pieces of wrapping twine she had saved from one of the stores uptown. When she was finished, she informed her students that on the coming Friday afternoon they would make a field trip to the Schminck Museum where they would present their buttons to Mrs. Lula Schminck. Mrs. Hull had discovered that Mrs. Schminck loved buttons and charged the admission price of one button for her pioneer museum.

The museum was located in the basement of Mr. and Mrs. Schminck's home It was within easy walking distance from the North School, as it was only a half-block south of the courthouse, up on E Street. It was a familiar street to Marie because it was the same street where Aunt May and Uncle Elmer, and Aunt Gladys and Uncle Kelt lived.

Marie fell in love with Dalph and Lula Schminck's cozy basement museum. Their basement was arranged to look like a typical pioneer home. String after string of colorful buttons were looped and fastened to the basement ceiling. There was a wood-fired cook stove, like the ones in the kitchen down at the grange hall, there was a pie safe with pretty designs tooled into the copper front, not like the plain pie safe out on Grandmo's back porch that was simply covered with fine mesh screening. There were beautiful quilts piled all around and tucked into the top of an old-fashioned bed. Everywhere you looked there was another item used by the settlers of olden days.

It was a matter of curiosity to Marie, on that day, as she noted that many of those items, or items similar to those on display at the Schminck's basement museum, were still being used at the ranch and by other neighbors out in Valley Falls. She guessed it was because they were country people and country people still felt like it was necessary to hold on to some of those old ideas more so than people who lived in town. In fact, it was almost a matter of pride for her that she knew what those items were and how they were used.

She thought about how she had overheard Ed Wright from up in Crooked Creek laughingly complain about all those new-fangled electric gadgets that his wife, Velma, had bought. How she heard him telling the other men down at the grange hall that when the electricity went out, he couldn't even go to bed to get warm because Velma had taken away all the old quilts and replaced them with an electric blanket!

Funny as his remark was, the truth of it was that the electricity often went out for several days at a time when severe winter storms blew down power lines. Velma, of course, like all the other women out in the country kept those quilts and other items such as kerosene lamps and wood-burning stoves handy for just such emergencies.

Marie was especially enchanted with the Schminck Museum because Mrs. Moffit, who was Marie's second-grade teacher, had introduced the students in her class to the "Little House on the Prairie" books by Laura Ingalls Wilder. Now, after experiencing Mr. and Mrs. Schminck's wonderful museum, Marie was forever in love with those long-ago stories of pioneer life! She thought it must have been fun to live in those days, but on the other hand, life was nice with electric lights, refrigerators, a washing machine that did not require stinky oil and gasoline, not to mention a wonderfully warm car in which to drive into town on a cold, winter day.

# One Season at a Time

The absence of Lytle Simms took its physical and emotional toll on everyone who lived and worked at the ranch beneath the rim. For months there was a continual grief that simmered where it lurked just below the surface. Beyond that they felt the loss of his down-to-earth, common sense knowledge about all things that pertained to the land and the livestock. There was the loss of his lifetime well of wisdom. Lytle was sixty-eight when he passed—not a young man and yet not so old either. The loss of his determination combined with Lottie's own force and will that the ranch would continue in a forward pattern no matter the obstacles that are bound to rear their ugly heads.

Before his passing Lytle himself had already experienced a change of mindset about the direction of the national agriculture economy in which lambs and wool were no longer in high demand.

There was also the loss of his physical manpower. Although age and health had already taken some toll on his body, to the best of his ability he had continued to work. Although he had ceased to ride horses and no longer took up his shovel and walked out over the ditches to divert irrigation, he still drove a tractor, a pickup and car. He was able to tally the lambs and he still stomped fleeces in the long sacks of wool when the sheep were sheared.

When the lambs were docked, he took care of small details like cleaning and disinfecting the docking shears as he stored them away for another year. It was all that sum total of little things, here and there, that they missed the most. And now it was up to someone else to remember to do those almost unnoticed little chores that until now they had taken for granted.

The last team of workhorses, Prince and Dolly, had already taken their retirement up in the buck pasture, behind the timber culture. By the time of Lytle's passing in 1952 they'd been up there for at least two years. Now the hay was raked with a side-delivery rake pulled by the little size-B Farmall tractor. The big size-M Farmall pulled the hay-baler.

Bucking bales of hay had been beyond Lytle's physical endurance clear from the beginning when the ranch had switched over to baled hay. Donald was constantly on the lookout for good hired men during summer's haying season. They weren't easy to find. Sometimes Laurney Young and Dale Wallace, who were married to Donald's cousins, Blanche and Bernice, came out on the weekends to help. Donald sure appreciated that.

Jack Barham, too, was an old man.

Every year it was about the first of June when 'ol Jack tied up his canvas bed-roll and boarded the mail-stage down at the Valley Falls Store to spend the summer working his mining claim up in the Blue Mountains of north-eastern Oregon. He usually stayed up there until the first snowfall.

In Marie's own memory, ol' Jack was always an old man with a full head of white hair and full white beard to match. To the best that anyone seemed to know, Jack never did learn how to drive a tractor or any piece of machinery let alone the pickup and so when lambing and feeding were over for the winter and spring, his ranch-hand abilities were mostly exhausted. Jack Barham was sure that there was still a "Mother Lode" of gold just waiting for his pick and his shovel to expose his gleaming fortune.

Year after year Donald enlarged the ranch's tillable land at a steady rate. Grain was in high demand in post-war America and the ranch had a good amount of bottomland that was prime for wheat, oats and barley. It was at his insistence that they had bought the little D-3 cat to break up fallow ground. That more powerful crawler tractor had more than paid for itself.

More fields of grain required a newer, larger combine to harvest the grain. The more machinery the ranch acquired the more need there was for a substantial shed to house the machinery from the ravages of winter and so a machine-shed was built out north of the big corral and the barn.

Donald knew that he had to press forward by modernizing and diversifying the ranch's natural and abundant resources.

Lottie, his mother, was still the majority owner of the ranch and there were times, after Lytle's death, that it was hard to persuade her that they must continue to look forward. Lytle's death had ravaged her soul and her spark for life flew away for a while. However, as time crept along her pain gradually grew duller and farther and farther back in her day-to-day conscience and eventually, week after week and month after month, Lottie began to reawake and think about the future for more than just one season at a time.

When it was all said and done, Lottie Simms wanted the ranch to thrive and prosper for Donald and for Donald's family.

Every year since back there in that fall and winter of 1949, when the bulk of the sheep were sold off, the amount of Simms Ranch cattle increased. Heifer calves were sorted out and carefully looked over. The heifers which they considered the most promising were kept back to use as future breeding stock. Unlike sheep, the more cattle they ran the more it called for building of more fence. Grazing land had to be rotated and regulated. Bulls had to be selected with careful thought as to their blood lines and with the increased use of government grazing allotments for cattle, bulls needed to be purchased from registered livestock producers.

The more cattle the ranch raised, the more the need arose for the ranch to acquire younger, stronger and an adequate amount of good saddle horses.

One by one the old sheep-camp horses had died off after serving their faithful last as steady and trustworthy mounts for sheepherders who plodded along behind slow moving bands, occasionally changing their course toward a greener pasture. Marie could remember old Skindawg, the last of those horses. She remembered his worn-out and bony, roan body hunkered up against the north wind as he stood in the shelter of massive English Poplar trees that bordered the south side of the orchard.

Donald's horse, Billy Sunday, also grew old and died. His uncle, George Chandler, gave Billy Sunday to Donald when Donald, himself, was no more than five years of age. Billy was an orphaned colt, hand-raised by his uncle's buckaroos. When he was a gelded yearling, George gave Billy to Donald. Donald and Billy grew up together with a fierce loyalty—each to the other.

Travel through time, however, is cruel in its inequality for man and his horse. The horse rapidly grows old while his human master remains in the youthful prime of his life and so the anguish of eternal separation must be suffered early by the master while the horse grows old and hurries on to its old-age and eventual death.

Darlene held Marie's hand as they followed Donald across to Grandpo's and Grandmo's house. They turned their faces to the south as they braced against a cold north wind. Inside Lottie's warm kitchen, Donald snatched a cup from the cupboard and poured himself a cup of coffee. His face was set and grim.

"I hated like hell to do it, but I kind of ignored how miserable 'ol Billy looked last night. I just didn't have the heart to face it."

Lytle turned in his chair where he sat, just off the kitchen, in Lottie's sunny and bright dinette as he said, "What do think, Son?"

"I can't stand it any longer. He's down by the haystack."

Lytle, grim himself, sighed, "I'll go down an' check on him."

Darlene entertained Marie with last summer's Montgomery Ward catalog. Marie used her grandmother's sewing scissors as she cut out dresses for new paper dolls.

Lytle went to the hall closet and took out his thirty-thirty. He grabbed his coat from a nail and picked up a clip of shells from amongst scattered and assorted items on top of the chest of drawers. Lottie busied herself as she began to wash up the breakfast dishes while Donald finally found himself a seat on the stool behind the warmth of his mother's kitchen stove.

Marie looked up at Darlene, "What's Grandpo gonna do with his gun?"

"Daddy saw a coyote down by the haystack."

"Oh."

They all made pretense at whatever it was they were doing while they waited and listened and waited and listened for the sound of a single gunshot. Marie knew that Grandpo would surely kill a coyote with one shot.

The sound never came.

Donald finally muttered, "What the hell's taking so damned long?"

Everyone turned when they heard Lytle's footsteps out on the front porch. It seemed like it took him forever to reach the front room door and turn the handle. Everyone looked at him with the same silent question.

"Ol Billy went to meet his maker in the middle of the night. He was cold an' stiff as a board."

As Lytle put the clip back on the chest of drawers and set his rifle in the closet, Donald said, "Thank God. I'll go drag his poor old body off. Somewhere out in the sagebrush."

Even before Billy Sunday died, Lytle had already bought a younger saddle horse. He was tall, a bit on the stocky side, and he was white. You couldn't say, "pure white" because there were flecks of light grey here and there. His name was "Silver" and as far as Marie was concerned, he was exactly like his name-sake, ridden by none other than The Lone Ranger. The first time that Grandpo tossed her up on Silver's back, Marie was thrilled. She was almost ready to throw her beloved stick horses away right then and there, but then, on second thought she decided to keep them around for a while longer.

Donald said that Silver was a good horse, "Tough as all get out for under the rim, but he has a hard mouth an' he's shore as hell hard to catch!"

No matter how small or large the enclosure was, be it the corral, the orchard or heaven forbid, clear down in the meadow, Silver had to be forced into a corner before he allowed himself to be caught. However, once a rope was around his stubborn neck, he was as gentle as ol' Tom, the house cat.

And then one day Blackie came to the ranch.

Blackie and Silver were about as good as horses can ever get. They weren't really in the category of just any ranch horse because they came to be almost like family. Back in those days it seemed like the ranch and Blackie and Silver just went together. The stories of Blackie and Silver, especially Blackie, could fill a good-sized book.

Marie never forgot them. Sometimes when she was a grown woman, and she lived far away from the old ranch, she would think about them, especially Blackie. She thought about those long-ago summer days when she helped Daddy gather cattle beneath Abert Rim.

She rode Blackie as she mused down memory lane. She smelled his warm sweaty horse smell. He was one horse that you could trust, anywhere, anytime. When she threw her leg over the saddle and jumped to the ground, she could throw his reins down and Blackie would stay put—right there. He would lower his head as his wise eyes looked at her and she looked back.

She didn't really stop to think all that much about the love of a good horse back in those carefree days, but somewhere, down deep inside, it was there. She took him for granted back then, and later she often wished that she would have taken the time and the thought to tell him how much he meant to her.

It was with Blackie that Marie learned how to saddle and bridle a horse. When she was still too small to put her foot in the stirrup and properly swing into the saddle, Grandmo taught her how to lead Blackie over to one of the boulders in front of the barn where she could swing into the saddle with ease. Blackie stood still and patiently waited while she learned the proper way.

There came a year when the ranch had more cattle than Daddy could easily gather by himself in one day. That year Marie became a buckaroo helper for Daddy as she learned how to gather the cattle and push them down the mountain and into the corral. She burst with pride one day as Donald told someone that she was, "his main buckaroo." In truth of the matter, she was his main buckaroo because, in those years before her brothers grew old enough to ride, she was his only buckaroo and Blackie, by himself, knew what to do when he got behind a cow.

Time never stands still and, that being the case, life went on at the ranch, one season after the next, with gaps filled here some, and there some in one way or another. The grief that Lytle Simms left with those gaping holes became duller and further away as the years passed by, but for those who knew him the gaps were never completely filled.

# Last Shuffle to the South School

Twin dust clouds rolled back from the jeep station wagon as Donald came to a stop beneath the shade of those grand old Poplar trees that lined the ditch bank in front of the house. He opened the door, leaned over and lifted Raymond out before he gathered the mail and headed for the house. There was a certain attitude about his step. It looked like he might be teetering on the verge of indignant or even downright mad.

Raymond, unconcerned about his father's mood, tarried behind. He picked up an interesting stick and dragged it through the gravel drive, then he plop, plopped the stick into the creek as he meandered across the plank bridge. He paid no attention to his parents' conversation that boiled over just inside the screen door.

"That's it. That boy 's got to have a regular hair cut! I mean it. No ifs, ands or buts about it!"

Darlene knew there 'd been trouble when she replied, "Well, next time we're in town one of us can take him to the barber shop."

"You can take him. I suppose you'll want to save some of those damned curls."

Donald, with barely controlled voice, rehearsed the scene he had just left down at the store.

Raymond sat, as innocent as a one-and-a-half, going on two-year-old, child can be on the old weathered oxbow that rested in front of Bessie Carroll's glass display cabinet. Donald pulled an Oly from the cold drink bin. He stepped out of the way as the woman of the young couple filling with gas out front walked up to the bin and drew out a soda. She looked down at Raymond with his gorgeous dark brown curls and exclaimed, "What a pretty little girl!"

And that did it! Darlene had held on to her baby boy's curls for as long as she dared. It had come to an end, because Donald Simms was not about to have his son mistaken for a girl.

A few days later a scene played out at the barber shop in town that made Marie wish that she was someplace else. Anywhere! What in the world had made her decide that she ought to go with Mamma and Raymond to the barber shop? She supposed it was because she'd never seen the inside of the barber shop before. Why didn't she tag along behind Grandmo as she went over to the Penny Store?

The barber lifted Raymond onto a board he had placed across the arms of his barber chair and the minute he did, Raymond began to kick and scream. Not cry—scream! The barber tied a clean cape around Raymond's neck as Raymond's screams grew into a sobbing wail.

Over the commotion Darlene tried to appear calm as she told the barber that she wanted Raymond to have a regular little boy's hair-cut.

Weakly, she apologized.

The barber said, "Don't worry about it. I've handled lots of first hair-cuts."

Raymond continued to kick and scream. Darlene did the best she could to hold him down while the barber took quick snips between flailing arms, legs and a head that bobbed, jerked and ducked. Tears mixed with running snot and snippets of curly brown hair got sucked into Raymond's mouth. He choked, gagged and threw-up all over the chair, the barber and Darlene.

Mortified at the scene Marie tried to shrink deeper and deeper into one of those red cracked Naugahyde chairs lined up for the barber's waiting customers along his shop's wall.

It took a full two months before Darlene dared tackle the haircut situation again. Donald was somewhat reluctant and gun-shy about the whole affair, but he said he'd give it a try. All that probably happened because Lottie stuck her nose in where it wasn't wanted, or needed, as she suggested that if his father took him to the barber shop, Raymond might act a lot better.

Lottie Simms was wrong. Dead wrong.

Moreover, Donald swore a blue streak that he'd never do it again. It was up to Raymond's mother and that was all there was to that.

About two months later, Raymond's lovely curls were showing quite nicely again. They had stopped in at Aunt May's house for something or other and that's where the discussion of who was going to take Raymond to the barber shop took place.

Uncle Elmer chuckled to himself and he turned to Raymond and said, "Young fella, how to you feel about walking uptown with me? We might stop by News and Sweets for an ice cream cone."

"Sure," Raymond said as he placed his hand in Uncle Elmer's and they walked out the front door.

About an hour later they returned. Raymond was calm, his hair was neat and precisely cut and he licked on a chocolate ice cream cone.

From that day on, Uncle Elmer Ahlstrom and Raymond had a monthly hair-cut date. After an approximate year had drifted by, Raymond's hair-cuts were no longer an issue as he had learned to behave quite nicely during his trips to the barber shop.

When school resumed that fall it was no surprise to Madge, Marie and Mike when they found themselves shuffled back down to the South School. They were fourth graders now and they oozed confidence in front of those new little first graders who were now riding the Valley Falls bus for the first time.

Down at the South School they would be able to watch progress as workers constructed a brand-new school—the Arthur D. Hay School.

It happened that the new school building was under construction on a vacant lot directly behind the schoolyard fence down at the South School. By the opening of school next fall, the Arthur D. Hay school would be ready for all of Lakeview district's fourth, fifth and sixth graders.

Donald didn't have time to fume and fuss over Marie's going back down to the South School, even though Miss Jennie Carroll, was still the principal. He had been outnumbered when she was shipped into Jennie Carroll's custody back in the second grade and in the end, everything had worked itself out. He had other things on his mind now, with his father gone, the ranch and now he was the master of the Valley Falls Grange and so he figured that one more year wouldn't make much difference.

From the first day of school Marie liked Mrs. Ludwig. She was a well-seasoned teacher, comfortable with her students, confident and kind, but firm to the point that she was not about to be intimidated by either her students or an administrator who, although might have had the best interests of the school at heart, came off as a dictatorial marshal. Mrs. Ludwig reminded Marie somewhat of Grandmo.

Mrs. Ludwig's fourth-grade class had been hastily added and thus it was crowded into the old basement section of the school. However, there were sufficient windows that poked out above ground level and Mrs. Ludwig had decorated her room with interesting and colorful penmanship banners, animal posters, photos of natural wonders and so her students, as well as she, soon forgot that the classroom was in the basement.

In 1952 Lakeview, Oregon was operating in the same frame of mind as was most of the United States. It was time to put away old-fashioned ideas and embrace prosperous modern times. It was, "out with the old and in with the new." In keeping with that, the school district decided that upon completion of the Arthur D. Hay building it was time to change the names of the other two elementary schools to something more significant than "North" and "South."

Arthur D. Hay had been a revered judge back in Lake County's history.

Lakeview's first buildings were hastily constructed on the donated homestead site of A. M. Bullard. His homestead was located at the mouth of Bullard Canyon right where Bullard Creek was diverted into an underground flume. Later, some thought that town site was a bad decision but, with the exception of an extreme warm rain following an extraordinarily heavy snow pack, Bullard Creek passes peacefully beneath most of Lakeview. Since Bullard's homestead was the beginning of Lakeview it seemed appropriate to attach his name to a school and so the old North School became Bullard School.

John C. Fremont was a famous explorer. Clear back before the days of the Civil War, back in 1843, Fremont passed through the middle part of Lake County giving names to places like Winter Rim and Summer Lake, up north, and to some of the lakes out in Warner Valley. Lake County's national forest land was called Fremont National Forest and so it was fitting that the old South School became Fremont School.

County officials talked more and more about the fact that the old Lake County courthouse was unstable and on the verge of being condemned. Architects said it was quite feasible to design a new courthouse in an L shape and construct it around the existing courthouse, which was in the center of the block. When the new structure was complete the old brick courthouse could be demolished without upsetting the flow of county business. It was sold to the citizens of Lake County as an acceptable idea. Afterall, a sleek modern courthouse in the center of Lakeview's business district would only enhance the appearance of a forward-thinking and prosperous community.

There were some holdouts, however, who held sentiment toward the stately appearance of the courthouse—the red brick matched other downtown buildings. Its clock tower and spires were the center of town, and what about the shade trees and lilac arbors that surrounded the courthouse? Were they not an inviting respite from summer heat? What would become of the water fountain? Where would children roller skate? What about the old bandstand?

Never mind, it was time to think about a modern future.

Through all that marching of time and prosperity Marie was growing older and she was expected to act like a young lady. Anyway, that's what Grandmo said, and she said it over and over.

Marie was on the fence about all that "young lady" business. There was a part of her that couldn't wait to grow up and there was another part that wanted to cling to her stick horses and even to dolls, although she didn't play that much with dolls. She had figured out that they made a nice decoration on her bed.

Grandmo had taught Marie how to make her bed and insisted that she do it every single day. Her girly bedroom had made a permanent move over to Grandmo's house now, and her little brother had moved into her old room in Donald's and Darlene's house across the drive.

Although her hair was thick and lustrous, Marie did not like its brown color. "I'd rather be blond, like Sharon and Madge. Why am I round instead of skinny, like them? I'm awkward. I'm no good at ball games and I can't swim."

It was during that summer before fourth-grade that Darlene finally cut Marie's long hair. Marie figured out that her mother must have liked her long hair because Darlene cut the braids straight off at the middle and put the braided pieces with red ribbons still tied to their ends away in a box that she kept on an upper shelf in her bedroom closet. When Marie discovered that she almost felt a little guilty.

But if she couldn't be blond at least she could have short curly hair. There was a problem, of course, because her hair was straight as a stick. Darlene went to Thornton's Rexall Drug Store and bought a home permanent kit and Mamma was quite successful with the stinky solution as she coaxed some curl into Marie's hair. Marie loved it. No more long tangles when her braids were brushed out; no more crying and Darlene's good humor tried to the hilt as she exclaimed, "Sit still, you're just making it worse!"

Another change that happened in Marie's life was that her mother was no longer "Mommy." Now she was "Mamma," or on more sophisticated days, which still didn't happen too often, "Mom."

And her father became "Dad."

There was something about Lottie Simms, however, because for her grandchildren, she always remained "Grandmo," with a long "O" at the end.

Mrs. Ludwig overheard Mike and Marie talk to the other kids about how they square danced on Saturday night at the grange hall. She got an idea that if Marie and Mike could teach the other children in her class to square dance it would make a good pioneer history lesson as well as good physical exercise after lunch. Probing with a few questions Mrs. Ludwig discovered that the children were quite adept at square dancing and even better, that Marie's father was a square dance caller.

Saturday nights at the Valley Falls Grange hall were some of the best entertainment ever. Almost everyone who lived in the valley came and most of the ranchers in Crooked Creek Valley. Many who lived in Lakeview had joined the grange, for both the grange insurance program and the Saturday night dances. Some even came down from Paisley. Valley Falls Grange meetings were held on the first and third Saturday nights of each month.

Granges were organized into local community granges: Fort Rock, Summer Lake, Valley Falls, Thomas Creek, Westside and East Side. The Pomona Grange included all the granges in the county and met one Saturday in each quarter of the year at one of the community halls. Granges held some political influence with the county, state and national legislative affairs in the agriculture world. The Grange, at both the state and national level, hired political lobbyists so rural members, especially, paid attention to the business meetings with serious intent.

The grange was also organized as a fraternal order with formal floorwork, signs, signals, passwords and symbols. Much of the early organization had been patterned after the Order of the Masons. There was a full spectrum of officers from the master down to the three graces, Flora, Pomona and Ceres. Substantial amounts of money were involved what with yearly dues and fundraisers for buildings and upkeep on those buildings so the offices of secretary and treasurer were held with grim responsibility. Wooden stations were set up in front of various officers and each officer wore a blue felt sash trimmed with gold—also in felt.

At the conclusion of each meeting the wooden stations along with the rest of the official paraphernalia were whisked away to a big closet down at the northwest corner of the hall.

Lottie Simms' next younger sister, Lora Newton, was the musician. When all the responsibilities of the meeting were stashed away, she trickled her fingers over the old upright piano's keys as she switched from rousing floor-work marches to lilting dance numbers and couples began to waltz over the polished hardwood floor. Her tempo gradually changed from waltz to two-step and after a couple of warm-up dances Donald stepped up on the platform where the piano held reign and called out, "get your partners and let's get squared up!"

Adults streamed onto the floor to make three full sets of square dancers and in the far corner, next to the dining room door, was a set of kids. Boys and girls had been taught a set of proper social etiquette skills so girls wiggled and squirmed on one foot and then the other while the boys quickly asked them to dance. They knew how to do-se-do, dip-n-dive, promenade and swing your partner as well as the adults and if it happened that adult sets were shy a couple, the kids filled in.

About midnight the dancing stopped for a potluck supper of sandwiches, salads, pies, cakes and cookies all washed down with coffee made in two-gallon granite pots on wood stoves out in the kitchen. The kids drank cool aide or maybe hot cocoa made in a milk-pan if it happened to be a cold winter night. Then dancing resumed until Aunt Lora played "Home Sweet Home" about two o'clock in the morning.

Down at the South School there was an empty room next to the furnace room and across the hall from Mrs. Ludwig's fourth-grade classroom. It was there that Mike and Marie attempted to teach their fellow class mates how to square dance. In Marie's opinion it was mostly a failure.

She came to school supplied with some of Daddy's calls but she couldn't make it sound the same way he did. There was a singsong quality to his voice when he called the patterns and there was enthusiasm – lots of enthusiasm for the fun he was having.

"Dip-n-dive an' go right under,"

"All eight swing an' swing like thunder!"

"Allemande left an' grand right an' left."

"Now do-se-do!"

"Dough, dough a little more dough!"

"Chicken in the bread-pan,"

"Kickin' out dough!"

With all that going on the winter of 1952 crept by. Christmas without Grandpo came and went and New Year's Day of 1953 dawned cold and bright. It was soon after the new year when Darlene told Marie some very exciting news.

# Mountains to Climb, Rivers to Cross

There was a whisper of change in the winter wind as it swirled and whistled around the eaves.

Lottie's inner core, her instinct perhaps, guarded her against the act of wearing her grief pinned to her sleeve. There were times and there were days when her heartbreak almost won the battle, but her stubborn nature was determined to not let the ravages of time declare a defeat. She continued to feel Lytle's presence in the house: in the kitchen as she cooked some little thing to eat, in the front room as she listened to the news broadcast over the radio waves and he was still with her in bed—beside her at night. He was there as she wandered about the corrals and the barn, as she listened to the musical trickle of the water trough, smelled the sagebrush and heard the breeze rustling through the trees.

As Lottie pondered his lingering presence in her life, she felt there were times when he talked to her, "You've got to keep it up, Kid. There are still things you must do. You're not finished yet. You have mountains to climb and rivers to cross. I will never leave you. I'll always be right here."

While Marie carried on in her nine-year-old innocence, the adults in her life welcomed those whispers of change they felt and heard in the winter wind.

Marie handed up boxes of Christmas decorations to Darlene who balanced at the opening of the attic storage. Darlene had pinned up the old curtain that covered the odd entrance to the attic space above the front room and kitchen. Once in a while Marie, herself, rummaged about up there as she carefully stepped from one exposed rafter to the other. She loved to poke through old forgotten stuff all of which she considered as precious treasures: old magazines, worn-out toys, things she had outgrown, Dad's old guitar. It was fun to pluck the sadly out-of-tune strings and pretend that she had a good singing voice, which she certainly did not.

"I have something to tell you."

As Darlene spoke to her daughter she strove for a casual tone in her voice.

"What Mamma?"

Darlene set the last box in its place and began to climb down. She smiled at Marie.

"About the first week of March you are going to get another baby brother or maybe this time it will be a baby sister. What do you think about that?"

"Oh! Oh! Mamma! I hope it's a baby sister!"

"Well, we'll just have to wait and see."

Now the winter began to drag as anticipation started to run high by the middle of February. It was not only Darlene who was expecting a baby, Virginia Crummett was expecting her first baby. The arrival of the new babies was approaching at almost the same time. Because it was her first baby and Virginia and Floyd had waited years for this baby the grange ladies held a baby shower for Virginia. Virginia and Floyd Crummett and all of their friends and family were very excited.

When Marie told Madge about the coming baby at the Simms ranch, they began to talk over names for Marie's baby sister. Both girls considered their own names to be either quite dull or completely odd and so it was that even before talk of the new baby they often considered what names were their all-time favorites.

Madge wasn't a bad name but it was so solid, so austere, so "down to earth." There was nothing imaginative about it. As for "Marie," well it was rather whimsical and very French, at least according to Marie's mother, but it was also the middle name of some of her cousins as well as many of her classmates and so she considered it rather common.

As a matter of fact, it was Marie's own middle name. Her first name was "Lottie," but for obvious reasons she couldn't be called by the same name as her namesake grandmother and Marie was glad about that because Lottie was so old-fashioned and, well—grandmotherly.

As they whiled away time on the school bus, they talked over their favorite names. Madge liked Patricia. Someone named Patricia would be a cute, fun-loving person that everyone would adore. Marie liked Irene. Irene was rather dramatic. A girl with the name of Irene would be glamorous and Marie, who considered herself the stark opposite of glamour, loved that idea. Of course, they kept this information secret between the two of them because they were only playing a game of pretend and besides that, in reality the baby could turn out to be another boy.

On target with her expected due date, Darlene checked into Lakeview Hospital during the first week of March. Virginia was already there and as it turned out she and Darlene shared a room. It seemed fitting. The two friends had graduated from high school together. It was through Virginia that Donald and Darlene met. Although Virginia's life had taken her from their little ranch on the banks of Crooked Creek to what seemed like a more refined life in Lakeview while Darlene's life had taken her from Lakeview to the ranch beneath Abert Rim, the two young women remained close.

Everything was on schedule and Marie was not surprised when she found her father waiting for her when school let out that afternoon. He was driving Grandmo's car. As soon as she got in the car, he said that he was going to take her up to Aunt Gladys' house. As he drove to Aunt Gladys Gunther's house up on E Street, he explained that Mamma was in the hospital. He said that Grandmo was up at Aunt Gladys' and Uncle Kelt's with Raymond.

As soon as they walked in the house Grandmo gave them the news that Aunt Ottie had called from the hospital to let them know that

Virginia had a baby boy. They named him Robert, she said, but everyone would probably call him Bobby.

Because Aunt Ottie Chandler worked in the laundry at the hospital and Aunt Pauline Chandler was a nurses' aide, hospital news that had anything to do with the family had a fast conduit to the rest of the Chandlers.

Dad hurried back down to the hospital to check on Mamma.

It seemed like a long evening and toward eight-thirty Donald decided he'd better take Lottie and the kids back out to the ranch. Raymond needed to be put to bed, he said, and Marie would have to be ready for school in the morning. He needed to help 'ol Jack. Jack would have the evening chores done and the dropping band in the barn, but he would need help to feed in the morning. Pauline was staying with Darlene and she'd call out to the ranch the minute there was any news.

Donald hated to have leave Darlene like this, but there was nothing else that he could do.

She'd told him, "Go on ahead. The kids have to be taken care of and you can't let things go at the ranch right now. I'm here in the hospital and everything will be fine."

The next day after school Dad was waiting again to take Marie back up to Aunt Gladys' house. Marie couldn't understand what was happening. By now she was old enough to know that babies didn't take this long to be born. She was scared, but she didn't dare to ask too many questions. She also knew that she'd get some non-committal answer that didn't tell her a thing.

All of the Chandler aunts: Aunt Gladys, Aunt Lora, Aunt May and Grandmo were huddled together—that's how they handled a crisis. They talked in hushed, worried tones. Aunt Lora said that she'd heard of doctors wrapping a woman's stomach with tape in this kind of situation. What was the situation? Marie didn't understand any of it, but she knew that it wasn't good. While they waited, she did her best to keep Raymond entertained.

There was no baby that day nor during the following night.

The next day at school Mrs. Ludwig said nothing to her about her new baby brother or sister, but the concerned teacher kept a careful eye on Marie and said nothing to the rest of the class.

Dad was there again when school let out. She shut the car door and gave her dad a worried look. He didn't start the car right away, instead he turned to face Marie and hesitating for a second or two he said, "Sister, there's something I have to tell you. Your mother's baby did not live."

Marie's eyes grew round and she was even more frightened with a mountain of unanswered questions.

"Mamma's alright. She's gonna be fine. When the little baby girl was born, yes it was a little girl, the umbilical cord was wrapped around her neck and it choked her."

Her baby sister had been choked to death!

"I want to see Mamma."

"You can't. The hospital won't allow children in the maternity section. I'm gonna take you back up to Gladys' house now while I see Mamma again for a little while an' then we're gonna go home for the night."

Days of grief began all over again.

It was different than when Grandpo had died—some of those days were worse and at the same time some of those days were easier because it went by in a hurried blur. Like a spark that ignites a wildfire there was a sudden explosion and everyone knew what had happened. The grange ladies got busy on the telephone as they spread the news and talked over what they could do to help out. Bea Brock lived in town and she said that she would go up to the Penny Store and get the prettiest and finest white baby shawl she could find and she'd take it up to the funeral home.

The next morning Donald took Marie down to the store to meet the school bus just like a normal school day. None of the kids said anything to Marie but they looked at her in a sad way so that she knew that they knew. Mrs. Ludwig put her arms around her as she entered the classroom; she gave Marie a hug, like a grandmother, and then the day went on like any other day.

As soon as Donald finished feeding, he cleaned up and went to town. He'd have to make burial arrangements. It was Friday so he hoped that they could have a simple graveside service tomorrow, on Saturday. He and Darlene had talked about it the night before.

When he'd brought it up, she turned her face to the wall for a second and heaved a quivering sigh. He hardly knew what to do but instinct made him take her hand. "I'm sorry sweetheart."

"I'm sorry as hell this happened, but we've got to take care of things."

She turned back to face him. Tears pooled in her eyes. She tried for a reassuring smile but it just wouldn't come. "How are Marie and Raymond?"

"Well Raymond doesn't know anything, of course, 'cept his mother isn't home. Marie's actin' brave. She doesn't really understand either, when it comes right down to it. I guess she was bent on havin' a little sister."

Darlene sobbed again. She tried not to, but she couldn't hold it in.

"Dr. Wilbur says I can't go home until next week. We can't wait that long to take care of things—have her buried. I'd like her buried there in the Simms plot. Maybe you could put her in the far corner opposite from Dad's grave. That way she'll be at my feet one of these days."

Donald couldn't stand it, tears streamed down his face, "Don't talk that way honey. It'll be years and years before we're, you and me, ready to talk about our own graves."

He knew she was sorer 'n hell and he shouldn't, or couldn't, move her too much. It was just that afternoon that she'd been through the horror that took place in the delivery room, but he couldn't help it; he reached down and gathered her into his arms. They clung together for a few minutes, and muffled against her shoulder he sobbed with her as he finally said, "I'll take care of things tomorrow honey—I'll do my best to make it like you want."

Mr. Osterman, the funeral director, showed him a beautiful white casket for a baby and Donald said that it was fine.

Just before noon with a heavy heart he found himself climbing the hospital steps again. As he opened the front door Darlene's sister, Wilma, was coming out. Wilma was crying and when she saw Donald her grief spilled over. He put his arms around her while she sobbed out, "She didn't get to hold her baby! She didn't even get to see her baby!"

He expelled yet another weary sigh. "I know Wilma, an' I'm sorry as I can be about it. Dr. Wilbur said they had some trouble gettin' her pulled together after the baby was born an' all and they rushed the baby right out an' up to the mortuary. He said he was real sorry about it afterwards, but it was too late to do anything about it then."

Then suddenly Donald had a thought as he said, "Well, I've got an idea. Maybe it'll help her out some."

He turned around then and walked back uptown to the newspaper office. He walked right back to his friend, Les Shaw's desk and plopped in the wooden chair Les kept beside his desk.

Les looked at Donald for a second and then he said he was sorry for what had happened. He supposed Donald wanted to put some kind of obituary in the paper. He'd seen some who did that, even when the baby was stillborn. Donald told Les about how it was that Darlene wasn't given a chance to see her baby and he wondered if Les would mind doing him a favor. Les nodded his head and said he'd take care of it. He'd call Osterman and just as soon as the baby was ready, he'd take his newspaper camera up and make a picture for Darlene.

Donald told Les that he really appreciated his doing that.

On Saturday morning, the Chandler family was gathered at Aunt Gladys' house before they went up to the funeral home and then on out to the cemetery. Donald sat at the table as he made out the papers for the baby's birth certificate. He shook his head and said, "We don't even have a name for her."

Grandmo, feeling helpless but thinking to be some help, spoke up, "I think in this case it would just be 'Baby Simms.'"

Marie could stand it no longer. Her sister must have a name. She rushed over to her father's side and with a boldness she seldom mustered up she said, "Dad, Madge and I have a name for her. We thought it was a perfect name."

Donald put his arm around her, "What name is that, Sister?"

"Irene Patricia. It's both of our favorite names."

"Well then, Sister, that will be her name."

They all stood beside little Irene Patricia Simms' casket in the funeral home for a few minutes before Mr. Osterman closed the lid. Her tiny doll face was framed with masses of brown curls just like those that her little brother, Raymond, had. Behind her, Marie heard one of the aunts say that she was a beautiful baby.

It was a small group that gathered beside the little grave out at the cemetery. They had on their winter coats but Marie never remembered if it was cold, or windy or if it was raining or snowing. She did always remember the day as being leaden and gray.

Donald had asked the Presbyterian minister to come. The minister said a few words and then he prayed. Then Mr. Osterman looked up, cleared his throat and said, "I guess that's it."

Then, all of a sudden, Aunt Gladys did something that she hadn't been asked to do, but she was determined to do it anyway. She stepped up beside the little casket and began to sing in a very soft voice, "Rocked In the Cradle of the Deep."

Donald brushed his face with the back of his hand. Then everyone turned and walked back to their cars. It made Marie feel better when her Dad reached down and took hold of her hand on their long, cold journey to Grandmo's green Kaiser, the car that they always kept clean inside and good for going to town.

# Mamma Comes Home

Darlene Simms was the most beautiful woman that Marie could ever remember seeing that day when her mother came home from the hospital. She never forgot how her mother looked—it was almost like she was a queen holding court as Marie saw Mamma sitting there in one of Bessie Carroll's captain's chairs beside the back counter at the Valley Falls Store.

When the school bus pulled up in front of the store Marie saw the back of Grandmo's car parked over to the side. She knew her father was waiting for her and she felt positively sure that her mother was there too. Grandmo's good car meant that he'd just driven out from town.

"Mamma surely came home today," she breathed to herself.

She could hardly stand it as the kids waited for Vest to pull the lever and open the doors. As soon as he did, she jumped down and raced into the store.

She ran headlong past Donald who was leaning against the counter passing the time of day with Herb Carroll. They were probably talking politics or something to do with the high price of something or the other. What difference did it make? There was Mamma.

Darlene held Raymond on her lap and he was gazing and smiling up into her face as though he had feared that he would never see his mother again and like a sudden miracle—there she was! She smiled her tender mother's smile as she gazed down at him. When Marie ran forward, Darlene held out her free arm and gathered her daughter tight.

Marie threw her arms around Darlene and buried her face in her neck.

"Mamma, Mamma," she sobbed and sighed.

Oh, the smell and the feel of Mamma!

Mamma wore her good silvery blue dress. The one with a dropped waist and a skirt that fell into shimmering pleats. Her thick dark-brown hair was pulled back from her face. Her hair looked almost black it was so dark, but in the light, there were glints of auburn that made it its true color of deep, deep brown. She wore the smallest trace of lipstick and rouge. That was all the makeup that Darlene Simms ever needed. Her complexion was a natural olive—a tone that others envied and longed for. Her cheekbones had just the right amount of height and her lips curved into perfection.

They drove on home to the ranch a happy and reunited family. They did, each one in their own heart, feel the loss of a baby, a daughter, a sister they never had the opportunity to know. But Donald and Darlene Simms planned to move forward. That's what they expected of her as well. It was unspoken, but she knew and they knew. Marie was old enough now. There was no time to dwell on what might have been or what was in the past, or even to talk about it. That's how you handled things during those years. At least it was the way the Simms family handled such horrid bumps in life's passage.

They expected that March would bring more blusters of snow, but each day as the snow went through its cycle of melt the grass and weeds underneath would show a grateful promise of green. One sunny day in April Darlene picked a bouquet of pussy willows from the old willow that grew beside the board-walk that went from the back door to the woodshed. When she put the little bouquet of pussy willows in a glass Mason jar and placed them in the middle of the kitchen table it was a definite sign that spring, as spring beneath Abert Rim is, had truly arrived.

Slowly but surely there was an increasing herd of cattle in the field up behind the barn. Newborn calves romped and played through slabs of baled hay as Dad eased the pickup through while ol' Jack pulled slabs off the bales and tossed them out.

Lambs were everywhere about the barnyard. All the lambing pens were full. As the lambs grew older and stronger, they were turned into bigger lots where they frolicked in groups and bucked and jumped with their long tails wringing and wiggling.

One morning Loyd Chandler came driving up from his place down on Crooked Creek. He stopped his pickup in the drive between the houses and his mother, Aunt Leona, got out. She went on in the house where she had a cup of left-over coffee with Darlene before Lottie finished up her morning chores and came over for a visit. Loyd hurried on out to the corral where Donald and ol' Jack were separating the sheep.

That day they planned to dock the lambs, give them an ear mark and neuter the males. Ol' Jack and Loyd pushed the sheep through the chute as Donald separated out the lambs into a small holding pen while nervous mother ewes in the big corral to the north of the barn began their frantic blatting and baaing.

If Marie allowed herself to give an over amount of thought to the business of docking lambs, she might have considered that it was a mean hard thing to do to such innocent little creatures. But she was a ranch girl and she knew that it was a necessary part of raising sheep. She knew that long tails on grown wooly sheep browsing on the open range was a dangerous and cruel notion. She knew that males had to be neutered and she knew that earmarks were part of a sheep rancher's legal ownership.

In all truth of the matter, she didn't think too much about it. She mostly knew that because it was a job that required extra help there was going to be an extra good dinner on the noon table.

When he was alive, Lytle Simms stored the docking shears in the tall wooden cabinet in his and Lottie's bathroom. The cabinet was painted a dull shade of green in high-gloss enamel so that it could withstand a thorough wash job every once in a while. The shears were mixed in with an unorganized assortment of livestock as well as human medical equipment and supplies. Because it still felt like the right place to keep the shears Donald, just as his father had always done, cleaned and sterilized them before he put them away for another year. Whenever Marie happened to open that cabinet and saw those docking shears, she gave a rather reactive shudder. The wicked looking curve on the end looked very doctorish, but just like unimaginable things that doctors were often required to do—the lambs had to lose their tails. It was part of life.

Loyd and ol' Jack used sheep-hooks as they pushed into the frightened flock of bunching lambs. When they snagged one, they grabbed the lamb and sat it on an extra-wide board nailed to the top of the corral fence. In a flash Donald docked the tail, then picked up his jackknife to cut a slit in one ear and took a nip off the other and just as quick he neutered the males. Then he dipped a round wooden peg into a pan of branding paint and dobbed a red dot on the lamb's back. Afterwards, when Marie was years older and she tried to remember, she pondered over whether the dot was placed on the neutered male lambs or on the ewe lambs. She couldn't remember which it was and she regretted that she never asked her father.

When they finished up, Donald counted the tails as he threw them in the pickup bed to haul off to the dump before the ranch dogs scattered them hither and yon. Then the men stopped by the watering trough to wash the top layer of blood and branding paint from their hands before they did a thorough wash at the house before they sat down to dinner.

With only Loyd and Aunt Leona extra there was plenty of room at the table for everyone to sit at the same time while they ate Mamma's roast beef, mashed potatoes and gravy, home canned vegetables and homemade rolls plus a piece of pie or perhaps a slice of cake.

On another morning, about the middle to the end of May, Loyd and Aunt Leona drove up again. It was early in the morning because Dad and Loyd had to ride out and gather in the small bunch of cattle. It didn't take long because Donald had kept them pretty close behind the barn. That day they branded the calves and then he turned them out to graze under the rim. When dinner was over Donald and ol' Jack went down to Loyd's where they gathered and branded their calves during the afternoon.

Aunt Leona always came with Loyd—even in the fall when he came up to go deer hunting.

Aunt Leona Chandler's life was often lonely for her after Uncle Heat died and then Virginia, her youngest child married and moved to Lakeview. One son, Loyd, never married and stayed to run the ranch while his brothers served during World War II, married and moved away to find other lives. All of the daughters married and moved to other locations. Aunt Leona's busy and boisterous household was now very empty.

The once hard-working woman with very few modern conveniences found aging hard on her emotional fiber and thus, for various reasons, she didn't like to stay in the house by herself for very long, especially if she knew that Loyd was away from the ranch. She was quite content in Darlene's front room. Lottie visited when she could but Aunt Leona didn't require anyone's special attention. Darlene had dinner to get on the table, plus she had to check on Raymond to make sure that he stayed out of trouble over at the corral. Aunt Leona simply settled into a chair, opened the wooden handles of her big cloth bag, dug around and pulled out some crochet thread, her crochet hook and watched everyone's coming and going, in and out of the house.

Loyd was always there for whatever it was about the Simms ranch that needed an extra hand. They were really just an extended part of the family.

Loyd and Aunt Leona were there each year when Johnny Armstrong brought his sheep shearing crew to the ranch. Johnny lived down in southern California and every spring he and his crew worked their way north as they sheared small bands of sheep. The ranch was down to about 250 to sometimes 300 ewes now so Johnny and his crew could easily get that amount sheared in two days.

It was usually about the first of June when Johnny arrived at the Simms ranch. Grandmo's birthday was June 1 and if Johnny happened to be there, he made a fuss about it at the noon dinner table.

Lottie blushed and flustered, "Oh it's just another day."

Johnny, in his singsong happy Mexican accent replied, "Not for a lady such as you, Mrs. Simms."

Marie liked to take her station up on the wool sacking platform so that she could watch the action below. Raymond climbed the ladder to the platform and jumped down into the long wool sack. He stomped around on the fleeces as Dad or Loyd, whichever one was doing the sacking, told him he was really helping out.

"How 'm I doin,' Loyd?"

Loyd threw another fleece down in the bag, "Here you go, tromp a little faster there, son."

Then Loyd let out his most favorite saying in the whole wide world, "Oh hell, you might as well have a kid on the job!"

Loyd laughed at Raymond and Raymond laughed right back at Loyd and stomped his little feet faster and faster.

Johnny and his crew laughed as they sheared and often, they broke in to one of their happy, rollicking native songs. When they finished shearing Johnny packed up his equipment while Donald figured the tally and wrote out a check. Before he left Johnny stood Marie and Raymond by a post in the shearing shed and marked off how tall they had grown since last year.

One afternoon late in May Donald came whistling up to the house. He set aside the fence panels to the backyard fence that went on past the woodshed so that he could plow the garden spot with the little B tractor. The newly turned-over earth was moist with a rich blackness that smelled of spring.

Marie's job was to help her mother work the soil into a smooth, rock free patch of perfection. She liked the sound and the feel of the garden rake as it pulled through the plowed soil. She liked that part. It was fun. But later on, the weeding and hoeing on a hot summer afternoon became somewhat tedious to Marie and she had to be coaxed into doing it. She couldn't understand why Mamma still liked it so much.

Darlene's garden was a masterpiece. Soon there would be radishes and wilted lettuce. Marie dipped her radish in salt before she bit into the crisp, sweet, tingly red and white splendor. Darlene cut up bacon, fried it crisp and made a dressing of bacon grease, vinegar and sugar to wilt the lettuce. The bounty of Mamma's garden with fresh fruits and vegetables, canning and preserves graced their dinner table all year long.

The best day of all was the last day of school. It always was, but the last day of school in 1953 for the fourth graders down at the South School was extra exciting.

On Wednesday Mrs. Ludwig announced, "Boys and girl, you know that Friday is our last day of school. I want each of you to bring a sack lunch and dress in work clothes and make sure that you wear sturdy shoes."

Their eyes opened wide. What could Mrs. Ludwig possibly have in mind? She, who was like all of their grandmothers rolled into one, certainly had something out of the ordinary up her sleeve!

She went on, "As you know, we have watched workers built a new school during this past year. Now it is almost complete, so on Friday, our last day of school, you are going to help as we move our fourth-grade text books and supplies over to the new school."

"Wow!"

"Oh Boy!"

She smiled at their enthusiasm, "*You*, boys and girls, will be the very first students inside the Arthur D. Hay school."

That was a good day. Even more so for Mrs. Ludwig, perhaps, than her students. They laughed and chattered as they lined up to carry as many books as their arms could hold. They oohed and awed over every bit of that shining newness. It was modern. It smelled so clean. The floors were so shiny they were almost slick. There was a whole gymnasium, with a locker room and a cafeteria too! When they were finished, happy and satisfied soon to be fifth graders gathered for lunch under the Maple tree on their old playground at the South School and Mrs. Ludwig brought out punch and cookies.

It wasn't long until Vest Carroll drove the Valley Falls school bus up for an early trip home. Marie and Mike scurried around as they picked up their lunch scraps and tossed them in the garbage. Quickly they promised their town friends that they were sure that they'd see them sometime during the summer.

"Good bye," Marie called to her in-town girl-friends. She'd probably see them for a few minutes if they happened to meet uptown, or maybe at the new swimming pool. Afterward they might troop down to the Polar Bear for an ice cream.

"Good bye, good bye," the town kids waved and called back as Vest started the bus and they drove away into summer.

# Blackie and Silver

Blackie was close to the best horse that God ever put on the face of this earth. He stood at medium height, his body was nicely rounded and as his name indicates, he was black. There was a small white star on his forehead. Donald claimed that Blackie was part Morgan. He velveted up real nice with a winter coat and when he shed off in the spring, he turned an outstanding amount of sleek.

Silver played second fiddle in Marie's affections to Blackie. Silver was white and thus a namesake for the Lone Ranger's great white horse. He was tall, stubborn when it came to being caught and his gait had a tendency to be on the rough side. Once caught, however, he was gentle as a dog. The Simms ranch version of Silver was nowhere the majestic quality of the Lone Ranger's horse, but all-in-all and in spite of his imperfections he was considered a darned good horse.

It turned out that both Silver and Blackie were good with kids which was a good thing because they were both ridden a lot by kids. During the prime of their lives, they were also quite adequate and dependable as ranch horses being well suited to the steep and rocky terrain beneath Abert Rim.

Later in her life when Marie began to ponder over bygone days at the Simms ranch it occurred to her that World War II had taken a chunk of her father's youth. Although Donald Simms was called up in the draft, he was given a hardship discharge after six months. Because he was an only child of a rancher whose health was in poor condition Donald was considered more of an asset to the war effort by working the ranch.

When Donald returned to the ranch from Fort Bliss, at El Paso, Texas, his company was about to ship out to the South Pacific. For several years, he talked often about the men he served with and wondered about them. It seemed to worry him some that he was safe at the ranch while he never knew what might have been the fate of some of the others.

In his early twenties he returned home from the army to a nineteen-year-old wife who was about to give birth to their first child. Darlene had followed him to Fort Sill at Lawton, Oklahoma, rooming and working off base until he was shipped to Fort Bliss. Nearing the last of her second trimester of pregnancy she returned to the ranch by taking the train across country to Klamath Falls.

Donald's and Darlene's new home was a single room above an old rock-cellar. The room had been hastily built after the old house burned and it had served as a bunkhouse until they married. Donald faced an entirely new set of responsibilities that included not only his new family but also the ranch and his mind was dead set on doing everything he possibly could for both.

After his return, Donald hardly took the time to look up from the wheel of his tractor as he broke ground for new fields of grain. He worked the sheep, keeping a constant eye out for sheepherders who were hard to find during the war and he tried to ease as many of his father's physical burdens as he could. He kept up that routine until the war was over. By the end of war, the habit of doing nothing other than ranch work was so ingrained in his nature that during Marie's earliest childhood she hardly remembered her father leaving the ranch for longer than one day at a time.

Marie could remember Donald's Billy Sunday horse, but in her memory the horse was very old and decrepit. She remembered the day that Billy Sunday died. Donald had loved Billy and he was such an intricate part of his childhood and youth that the loss of Billy Sunday was hard for him. Donald was not interested in raising and training another good horse.

Jack Barham kept a few of his horses around the ranch but neither Donald nor Lytle were impressed with them. As far as they were concerned ol'

Jack had spoiled them for anything useful with his lack of patience and his bad temper that often resulted in cruel treatment.

Marie also remembered an old sheep camp horse they called Skin Dawg. Skin Dawg wasn't good for anything other than packing the sheepherder's daily essentials as he drowsed along behind the sheep. Skin Dawg, like his name, was no beauty. She remembered him as a skinny old, old, very old roan that Grandpo found dead one morning under the spreading English Poplar tree that grew beside the orchard.

It was back even before Skin Dawg died that Lytle began to insist that they ought to find another horse. With very little enthusiasm Donald said, "fine."

Lytle found Silver at a place out on the Westside. He liked the looks of the horse and the price was right. When he told Donald about the horse, Donald replied, "If you think he's a good horse go ahead and buy him."

And Lytle did.

Marie was thrilled the day that Silver came to the ranch. The minute Grandpo unloaded the horse he threw a saddle on Silver's back, turned around, picked up Marie and placed her in the saddle. She was on a horse. A real horse.

The Lone Ranger had long been her favorite radio program and as she recreated those scenes, she galloped her stick horses with reckless abandon across the barnyard lots. She was the Lone Ranger and Tonto rolled into one person as she fearlessly rode the great horse Silver and also Scout—both at the same time.

"Hi Ho Silver," she shouted.

She immediately followed with, "Get 'em up Scout."

"What's his name, Grandpo?" she asked, as she sat atop their very own real live great white horse.

"Silver."

She knew it! She just knew it!

Darlene stood by, smiling. Lottie turned and went back in the house to bring out her Kodak and then she took a few pictures. Donald leaned against the side of his old tan Chevy. He tipped his grease splotched hat back on his head and grinned in spite of himself. He had to admit that, after all, they did need the horse.

He straightened up, walked over and took the reins from Lytle. He gave Silver a few gentle pats, ran his hand over the horse's rump, pulled his mane over straight and said, "Looks like a good horse."

Not long after Silver came to the ranch Lytle returned again from his and Lottie's weekly trip in to Lakeview and Lytle told Donald that he'd heard some news about another horse for sale. This horse was at another place out toward the Westside and he drove out to take a look at the horse.

"He's a hell of a good horse," he told Donald and he thought Donald ought to see the horse for himself.

"He's a good-looker alright enough," Donald thought to himself when he first saw the black horse. "Gentle as a dog."

The owner's kids brought the horse around to the front of the house with nothing more than a rope slipped loose around his neck.

At Donald's surprised look the man said, "The kids ride him all over the place but he's got more get an' go than I can use an' I really don't have any need for him. It's not often that you find a young horse like him an' at the same time you can catch him anywhere. You won't find a mean bone in his body."

After they loaded Blackie and drove away Lytle remarked, "I almost felt like a heel takin' him away from those kids."

Donald answered, "Yeah. That's about how I felt."

"Beauty is skin deep" so they say and in Blackie's case it was true because his value ran far deeper than his good looks.

"Easy to catch" was an understatement. If someone so much as laid a hand on Blackie he would follow anywhere.

It wasn't long until Donald took to riding Blackie almost every time that he needed a horse. Silver resisted being caught to the maximum amount possible. It usually took more than one person to force him into a corner before he submitted to a rope or a halter. Once caught, however, he was meek as could be, but because Blackie was so easy to catch Silver often roamed free in the meadow while Blackie's home pasture was in the orchard behind Donald's and Darlene's house. Blackie was quite content there because it was easy for him to investigate whatever was going on in the backyard.

Summer of 1955 was glorious. The crisp high-desert night air quickly warmed as the morning sun began to play peek-a-boo over the eastern edge of Abert Rim. Poplars, elms and maples spread shade across the drive between Lottie's and Donald's and Darlene's houses and filtered the summer breezes that fanned over the spacious lawns of both homes.

Wallace Creek trickled beside the drive as it passed on out to the barnyard where the Rehart Trail Creek joined its force to provide irrigation to the meadows below. The location of the ranch with its gravity flow spring system, tiny, but continuous, streams of water trickling beside the houses and through the barnyard, rich green lawns, bushes, shrubs and spreading shade trees were the envy of those who lived in the dryer and seemingly flatland of the valley below.

Aunts, uncles and cousins from town often drove out for Sunday afternoons, birthday celebrations, Fourth of July or for whatever else granted an occasion. When the cousins arrived, Blackie was quickly brought on deck. Blackie was content to go along with the plan because for him it was always a game and he liked to play games.

As many kids as would fit, climbed on Blackie's back. He slow-poked away from the barn. No amount of kicking or yelling changed his pace. He lumbered out to the gate that was about a quarter to a half-mile down the road along beside the alfalfa field. The forward rider tugged a dull-headed Blackie (who usually neck-reined when a serious rider was in the saddle) slowly, slowly around for the return trip. At sight of the barn Blackie's ears perked up, his nose thrust forward and it was as though his thought process transferred to his riders, "You'd better hang on kids, because now we're gonna have some fun."

He raced for the barn and everyone laughed as they ducked in unison just before he skidded under the overhang in front of the horse-barn door. Blackie's passengers piled off and the next bunch got on. Blackie was willing to play that game for hours.

Sometimes when Donald was in a particularly jovial mood he would meander out to the barn and show off his "Gene Autry mount." He backed a good way off from Blackie's rump, broke into a sudden run and leapfrogged over Blackie's rump into the saddle! Blackie was game for it, threw up his head, wheeled around and they ran at breakneck speed to the edge of the corral and back.

During that fall before the summer of '55 it was the first year of the Arthur D. Hay School and that fall Marie was in the fifth grade. Everything about school that fall was a new experience. There was a new class called Physical Education, or PE for short. Darlene went to the Penny Store and bought Marie's gym clothes—navy blue shorts and a white shirt. Marie had never worn shorts before. Other girls wore them and she admired them but she never had nor even dared ask to own such a piece of clothing.

Those gym shorts opened up a whole new world of modern ideas for both Donald and Darlene Simms and even Grandmo had to give in to a sign of the times in which they were living.

Girls played volleyball and basketball. They learned how to shed their modesty and strip down buck-naked in front of the other girls and run through a six-person shower as fast as possible. They soon figured out how to get just far enough under the shower heads so that they were wet enough to satisfy the gym teacher and still not mess up their hairdos. The gym teacher stood by the shower and made a check mark beside each name on her clipboard as the girls raced by to the dressing room.

Miss Ida Stroda taught a good fifth grade class. She opened their worlds a bit further as they began to explore social studies and science. Fractions expanded into decimal points. Math, beyond simple addition, subtraction, multiplication and division began to make more sense to Marie. Reading and spelling exploded into grammar, punctuation and the dreaded diagraming of sentences.

By mid-April the PE class moved outdoors to the school playground for dodge ball and soft ball.

As the spring of 1955 took firm hold on the ranch the prospect of another summer burst into bloom.

By that spring, Marie had lived with Blackie and Silver as part of her life for several years. Now that was about to celebrate her twelfth birthday, she considered herself an adequate horsewoman as she strode with confidence to the orchard to catch Blackie. She tossed the saddle blanket on his back, swung the saddle up and over, reached under his belly, grabbed the cinch and quick as a wink tightened the cinch strap. Blackie puffed up his belly and she jammed her knee into his gut. Then he whooshed out his breath and she finished tightening the cinch. Blackie clenched his teeth and tossed his head at the bridle's bit but it was more show than anything else. Silver actually put up less fuss about the bridle and seldom blew out his gut. Once caught, Silver was more practical about the bridle, but with Blackie it was a game.

About the middle of May it came time to brand the calves. Besides Loyd's help, some of the men from town liked to come out and help with the branding. Their wives usually came along too and more and more branding became a springtime celebration.

It was during that spring that Donald grumbled about how it was getting to be more than a one-person job to gather the cattle.

Marie piped up, "I can help."

Donald narrowed his eyes. He was a bit skeptical, but on the other hand he knew that she handled either of the horses quite well.

"Well hell, they're both so damned gentle anyway," he said to himself, "what harm can it do to let her try."

Out loud he said, "Well Sister, if you think you can help gather cattle be ready first thing in the morning."

It turned out that Marie *could* do it. It might be more accurate to say that she stuck to Blackie's back while he pushed cows down the Rehart Trail but nevertheless, Marie learned how to help Dad and the better she got at it the more he began to rely on her. Donald figured that he knew all along she could do anything she put her mind to, but her mother and her grandmother were not entirely convinced. What had become of their little girl?

It wasn't so much that they didn't think she could do the job as it was more that they felt fairly certain that Marie would never stick to her newfound buckaroo job. She would never continue even if she lasted for the day—it was a whim.

This was the girl who worried about how she was dressed. Their now girly little girl who loved her newfound curls that Darlene produced from the stinky solution of a permanent wave kit. The girl who more and more talked about how free of dust and mud were the neat, up to date, modern homes of her in-town friends. She was even a little snobbish about that somewhat to Darlene's dismay.

Ranch style housekeeping is in a category all of its own, and the Simms ranch was not an exception. Darlene's kitchen counters were covered with sterilized beer and pop bottles ready for the next feeding of bummer lambs. There was a whole collection of Donald's dusty, grease-stained hats and gloves on top of the refrigerator. The furniture was well-used and sometimes covered with dog and cat hair and it was a long wait until that furniture was replaced with something newer and more in style. There was scattering of sawdust and chips around the wood stove. If the weather was good, their laundry hung on the clothesline between the woodshed and the bunkhouse.

Marie's feminine bedroom in Grandmo's house was nice, thanks to Lottie's pampering of her granddaughter. But the twin beds weren't matching. The bathroom was right off the kitchen. A big clawfoot bathtub was the centerpiece and there was that ugly green cabinet with all the livestock doctoring equipment right there in the bathroom.

Marie often forgot, however, about how her town friends liked to come out to the ranch. How they liked the horses, the wonder of baby calves and lambs, traipsing through the barn and all things about the ranch. They thought *she* was the one with the wonderful life.

Darlene and Lottie thought that one day's worth of saddle sores and a good dose of sunburn would cure her, but they were wrong. She was willing to go back for more and the more she worked at it the better she became. It is true that God might not have intended for Marie to become a top-hand horsewoman, but He did not overlook her inborn, stubborn determination to finish a job once she got started.

After branding it wasn't long until school let out and it was about that time when Marie made a discovery that she felt should have been obvious to her but for all of her new found grown-up ways, she had missed it.

Aunt Lora and Uncle Harry Newton came out from town one Sunday and Marie walked into Grandmo's kitchen in the middle of a hushed and worried conversation between Grandmo and Aunt Lora.

"Aren't they worried?" Aunt Lora asked Lottie.

"Well, they don't say much," Lottie answered.

Then Lottie went on, "The baby's due the first week of August. We just have to leave it to the providence of the Good Lord."

Of a sudden Marie's head went dizzy. Mamma was pregnant.

Oh *please,* she began to beg God in heart. She wasn't even sure she knew who God was, but Grandmo seemed to know. She was prone to talk about the "Good Lord" quite often.

"Please," she begged Grandmo's Good Lord, "please let everything be alright this time. I don't care if it's a brother or a sister, I'll take either one. I just want Mamma to be alright and the baby born okay."

# Sonny

Grandma Brown sent a shock wave through her family one fall. It was back in 1953, during the fall after that dreary spring when Darlene had lost her baby. If Darlene had thought about it, which she did not, she would have considered herself strong and resilient. However, she could not bring herself to come face-to-face with her mother's new life. Afterwards, when it was all over, Darlene began to feel ashamed of herself and by the next spring she decided that she ought to do something about it.

Darlene didn't get many letters from her mother so when Donald brought the mail in, she grabbed the envelope right away, slid her thumb under the flap and gave it a jagged slash. As he fumed over the co-op bill Donald began to notice her sudden silence. He looked up and asked, "What's your mother got to say?"

"She's getting married next month and she wants us to come."

"Married? Your mother? Who 'n the hell is she going to marry?"

Darlene's father, Bert Brown, had been dead for several years and she had never thought about the possibility of her mother ever considering marriage with another man.

"His last name is Pullen. His wife died a couple of years ago. The odd thing is that he lives in the same house, right there in Cave Junction, where Mama and Daddy were living when Daddy died. Mama's going to wind up living in that log cabin across the road from the church. They're going to be married in that little church. The same church where we had Daddy's funeral."

Donald couldn't tell for sure. Was she in a state of shock? Or was she tending more toward being upset? He could not read his wife's mind.

"What do you want to do? Do you want to go?"

"No, I don't."

"Well it's whatever you want to do, Honey. If you want to go, then we'll go."

"No. No. You'll be busy with fall plowing. The wedding's on a Saturday afternoon and we'd have to take Marie out of school for a day an' all. We're just too busy."

No more was said about Grandma Brown's wedding. Marie thought about how it was that Grandma Brown would not be Grandma Brown anymore. She thought weddings were for young people. She and Raymond were simply two in a crowd when it came to Grandma Brown's grandchildren so none of them were overly attached, like they were with Grandmo, their grandmother Simms because they were the only grandchildren that Lottie had. Marie couldn't understand why someone as old as her Grandmother Brown would want to get married anyway.

She was sure that Grandmo would never go and do such an outlandish thing. Apparently, her mother felt the same way.

Early in November Darlene received another letter from her mother. This time it was a thick envelope stuffed with wedding snapshots.

"He looks like a nice man," Darlene mused to herself. Looking at the pictures, Darlene realized that she and her family were the only ones who did not attend her mother's wedding. Out of Hazel Frank Brown, now Pullen's, eight children Darlene was the only one missing.

Darlene spread the pictures on the kitchen table and thought about her father. It occurred to her that she probably had had a closer emotional connection to her father than to her mother.

Darlene thought back about how her mother had always been so busy. It wasn't easy to tend a garden, can and preserve food, sew clothing, cook, clean and wash for eight children plus herself and Bert. There was no time for hugging, kissing, soothing and other touchy-feely emotions once her babies were out of diapers and finished nursing. When Hazel's long days had come to their work-filled end it felt to Darlene like it was her father, Bert, who had had enough energy left over for a touch, a little squeeze or perhaps an encouraging word.

As she looked over the snapshots taken at her Mother's wedding Darlene's mind wandered to that long-ago day when she and Donald had announced to their parents that they were going to get married. When they told Lottie and Lytle about their plan to marry, Lottie immediately sat down at her desk and wrote out an invitation to dinner on the next Sunday for Bert, Hazel and their family. There were many ways in which their families were completely different, and yet, on the other hand, hard work and love of family were the core centers of both the Lytle Simms family and the Bert Brown family.

Lottie and Lytle had scrimped, saved and done everything they could do to keep the ranch beneath Abert Rim financially afloat. Hard work and doing without was part of their day-to-day living. On the other hand, no matter financial depression, drought or looming due dates on loans held by the bank, the ranch had always been there, solid, in one of God's chosen locations where food and shelter were ample. Donald Simms had never gone hungry or without a warm roof over his head nor had he ever worn a threadbare winter coat.

Bert and Hazel brought the younger half of their wanting family out of Nebraska to Lakeview, Oregon during the summer of 1941. Darlene had two brothers, including her twin brother, Darrel, and five sisters. Her older brother and two sisters were already married. Bert had done the best he could while working for other ranchers and farmers in South Dakota and Nebraska, but the combination of depression and drought had ruined most of them.

Hazel's brother, Amsey Frank, who had already moved out to Lakeview, wrote a wrote a letter back to Hazel that if they could find a way to get out to Oregon, he was sure that Bert could get a job in one of the sawmills.

"Things are good in Lakeview," he wrote.

By the summer of 1942, Bert Brown and his family were well on their way toward a better life in Lakeview. They still lived in an unpainted rough board cabin, down in the south part of town, but they had a milk-cow, a flock of chickens and Hazel was growing a large garden. Bert had a good paying job at the DeArmond Brothers sawmill.

The fact of the matter was that both the Simms family and the Brown family were country folks, doing the best they could with what they had. The Simms family, however, had the distinct advantage.

That Sunday evening in mid-August after he and Hazel had met Lottie and Lytle Simms for the first time, Bert sat beside Darlene on the front step of their cabin. The door behind them stood open to let in the cool evening air. Inside, Hazel tidied up and prepared for Monday morning as Darlene's younger sisters giggled over their day and got ready for bed. For a while, neither Bert nor Darlene had much to say.

Finally, Bert heaved a sigh as he reached over and patted his daughter's knee. "I'm right proud of you, Darlene. I'm glad that you stayed with school an' graduated. I expect with the war now an' everything else in consideration you'll wind up bein' the only one of us that gets that accomplished. That young man you're going to marry, Donald, he seems to be mighty fond of you an' his folks are good people. You'll be makin' your home in about as fine a place as I've ever laid eyes on. You're a mighty lucky girl."

As the memory of her father washed over Darlene, tears spilled out and ran down her cheeks. She gathered the pictures and placed them back in the envelope. "When spring comes," she thought, "I'd better pull myself together and go see Mama."

As things turned out, she didn't go in the spring. Once again, they were too busy. But the hay crop was short that summer and a good time for a few days spent away from the ranch often came after the haying was done and before the grain was ready to be thrashed.

One day at the noon dinner table Donald spoke up, "If you still want to make a trip over to Cave Junction, we ought to get ready an' go. Can you be ready to leave on Saturday?"

Darlene answered in the affirmative and Marie squirmed with joy in her seat. "We're going on a trip!" her mind squealed but her table manners came to the rescue in time for her to keep an outward appearance of calm and some semblance of politeness.

Lottie ate dinner with them every day. It was a ritual that Darlene had started after Lytle passed away. It was also an unspoken assumption that Lottie would go along on their trip. That's how they were as a family unit and no one ever questioned it. Afterall, they would travel in Grandmo's good car and probably Lottie would finance a portion of their adventure.

And so, it was not questioned when Lottie put in her opinion, "If you think there's enough time we might as well go on over to the coast for a couple days being's how we'd be that close anyway."

"Boy oh boy! A trip to the beach too!"

Because there weren't many places to stay if they drove on over to Cave Junction, they checked into a motel in Grants Pass. Everyone laughed at Raymond because he called it, "Grant's Pants" instead of Grants Pass. They spent all day, Sunday, with Hazel Pullen and her new husband.

It seemed kind of funny to think that she wasn't Grandma Brown anymore and although Marie called Hazel "Grandma" it still seemed a little strange.

Mr. Pullen was a very nice man. No one was able to address him in any other way. He was a quiet, polite man who asked Donald lots of questions about the ranch. He still worked his own little farm and Grandma was very cozy and content living back in her quaint log cabin home. She showed off her abundant garden. She hugged Marie and held Raymond on her lap, she couldn't seem to get enough of visiting with Darlene while Donald and Lottie found interesting things to talk about with Mr. Pullen.

Grandma cooked a fabulous Sunday dinner with bounty from her flock of chickens and her garden.

By some consequence that Marie never understood, Aunt Wilma, her husband, Troy Icenhower, and Marie's cousin, Inez, were living in Cave Junction at that same time. Iney came over to Grandma's house right after dinner and told Marie that a neighbor down the road had a television set.

"Wow," Marie said, "I've never seen a television."

They were seated side by side on Grandma's back step gnawing away on chunks of raw rhubarb which Iney claimed was very good but Marie never could get the hang of liking the sour taste.

"Mrs. Rinehart," (that was the neighbor lady's name) "she said I could bring you over to her house this afternoon because there is going to be something shown on the tv."

Darlene said that she could go and so the girls scampered down the dirt road to Mrs. Rinehart's house. At a quarter to three Mrs. Rinehart turned on the television for the test pattern to appear. Iney explained to Marie that you had to look at the test pattern for fifteen minutes before the television actually worked. and at three o'clock on the dot—just like magic—there it was! It was Adlai Stevenson giving a talk about how he should be elected President of the United States. Marie could hardly wait to tell her family about it!

She finally got to share her story while they were driving back to the motel.

Dad teased at Raymond while he was driving, "Where 're we goin'?"

Raymond piped up, "Grants Pants." Everyone laughed and Raymond couldn't figure out why.

When Marie got her two cents in about the television and Adlai Stevenson's grand talk, Donald grunted, "Humph. He's one of those 'Damn Cats.'"

When it came to politics the Simms family was Republican.

Spring of 1955 gave off signals that hot dry weather loomed ahead for summer. By late July those indications proved right.

Darlene rested, as much as her advanced pregnancy would allow. She sat in a lawn chair beneath shade provided by the large English Poplar trees that lined the eastern edge of the orchard and just below a wide expanse of lawn spreading north from the house. Outwardly she appeared calm, but inwardly she was mildly troubled. Ice cubes tinkled as she swirled her glass slowly around and around while her mind continued to wander over the past two years.

With eight children her mother had many grandchildren. Hazel Frank Brown Pullen had long ago ceased to be present for the birth of each grandbaby. She hadn't come when Raymond was born. His birth was in the winter, of course. She wasn't there when Darlene lost her baby girl. Afterward, she'd written to Darlene that if she'd had any idea how badly it would go, she would have been there. But how was she to know? Darlene didn't expect her mother for the birth of this baby either.

She was keenly aware of what made her so uneasy this time. It was natural she supposed, but if the truth were to be told Darlene longed for some way, anyway, that her mother could come. It wasn't going to happen. That was a fact. She had to put all this nonsense out of her mind.

There was an uneasiness about her mother, however, that Darlene couldn't let go.

"It's just because of the baby," she said to herself.

Her thoughts continued to wander, "It's so terribly hot. Donald's like a mad bear. He's trying to get the haying finished before the baby comes an' he needs help. Dale comes out in the evening when he gets off at the post office an' on the weekend. Thank God Dale and Bernice are back living in Lakeview. Thank God Bernice is at the hospital. I think I'm going to need her."

Bernice was Donald's cousin, his Aunt Gladys Gunther's daughter. Bernice and Donald shared a special relationship and after the war her husband, Dale Wallace, had become Donald's friend. During the war Bernice gave up nursing school, but now she was working at the hospital in town. She planned to become a full-fledged registered nurse, one of these days, when things got better.

Darlene thought about how Lottie had thrown a regular ring-tailed conniption fit yesterday afternoon.

Lottie was driving the truck so Donald could load the bales of hay without having to drive up, stop, climb on the truck bed to stack the bales and then do it over again and again until he had a truck load. Lottie went to the house for a glass of cold water while she waited for Donald to pick her up for the next load. For some reason Lottie decided to walk back out to the stack yard and there she caught Darlene wielding a hay hook as she pulled heavy bales of hay into the elevator.

As soon as Donald got the bales down a couple of layers on the truck Marie was dragging them to the edge where Darlene took over and pulled them on to the conveyor belt. Lottie hadn't realized their system and when she saw Darlene, big with child, tugging on heavy bales of hay she screamed, "What on earth are you doing? Stop that! Right now!"

And that was the end of that. It was possibly the reason that all of the hay was not out of field and stacked when Darlene gave birth to a beautiful, healthy baby boy a few days later on the third of August.

That evening at the hospital Donald asked Darlene what she wanted to name their new son.

Darlene answered, "I want him named for your dad and my dad, Lytle Albert."

It took Donald a second or two and then he replied, "That's quite a mouthful for such a little guy."

"I know. But he's the last chance we'll have to remember them that way."

Whether he was as beautiful as everyone raved on that he was, or if he was beautiful because everyone was filled with such blessed relief remained an unanswered question. Marie thought he was about the prettiest baby she'd ever seen.

Her mother spent hours holding him, looking at him and cooing her mother's love to him. Often Raymond leaned against his mother, looking too, because he couldn't seem to get enough of gazing at his little brother. Marie sat on the big round footstool, as close to her mother as she could get, elbows on her knees, chin propped in her hands as she watched and gazed upon this miracle.

Marie and Raymond took turns letting Lytle Albert grasp their fingers. They smiled at him and very softly called him Little Brother.

They loved to talk to him, "Little Brother look at this," or when he cried, "Oh, Little Brother, what's the matter?"

Darlene became horrified when she realized that her son was going to be called "Brother." For various reasons she did not like that name. She began to reprogram her other two children by calling her baby, "Sonny," or even her, "Little Sonny Boy."

Darlene's system worked and before long everyone in Lytle Albert's life began to call him "Sonny."

The remainder of that summer was wonderous and happy as it gradually rolled into what felt like a glorious fall.

Early one Saturday morning Marie sat on Grandmo's front-room couch as she slowly sorted through her rather extensive collection of comic books. Marie was one of Thornton's Rexall Drug Store's regular customers at their comic book racks located between the drug store area and their floral shop to the back. Lottie said that she was getting sick and tired of them piling up and scattered all over the place. Marie needed to get rid of some of what Lottie called, "those idiotic Jughead, Archie and Fritzy" comics.

The telephone on Lottie's living room wall jangled out the Simms ranch ring. Marie was so languid about the comic book sorting that, for once, Lottie reached the phone first.

"Hello."

Marie's interest perked up when she heard Aunt Wilma's voice filter out from the receiver.

"Mrs. Simms, I've got some awful bad news for Darlene. Mama's dead. Mr. Pullen found her out in the garden."

Marie gasped, jumped up and began to run for the door, "I'm going to tell Mamma."

Lottie grabbed the back of her blouse before she made it through the door.

"No, you don't young lady! You just stay put!"

Marie was as startled at Grandmo's uncharacteristic behavior as she was at the news that Grandma Brown was dead.

Lottie held Marie with a firm grip while she deciphered the details from Wilma.

She turned to Marie, "You know better than to do something like that. Your mother needs to hear this from me. Better yet from your dad, but he's down in the field. You run find him and tell him to high tail it back to the house as fast as he can."

# The River of Life

Junior High students were the Goslings to Lakeview Senior High's Honkers when the future graduating class of 1961 moved up from the Arthur D. Hay School to Junior High. Lakeview's Junior High was located on the top floor in the old section of the high school building.

Seventh and eighth grade students have always found themselves in an awkward, in-between condition. By the time children have progressed to twelve-years-of-age no one is in the mood to consider those awkward gangling youngsters as innocent little kids, and what's more, they consider themselves as having advanced above such childish treatment.

Parents, grandparents and teachers yell at middle school students and tell them to, "act your age."

Seventh-graders who have suddenly been pushed from the nest are not exactly sure what age they are supposed to be acting like. Becoming a certified teen-ager has been the ultimate dream, so far, of their life's desire. On the other hand, associating with high-school students scares the living hell either into or out of them.

Back in the 1950s the Valley Falls bus stopped by the side door of Lakeview High School where seventh and eighth grade students departed the bus and ran quickly up the back stairs to their sanctuary on the top floor. For the first two weeks of September new seventh-graders tread softly. Ever mindful of their elders.

Elders who, in other words, were the high school students who lurked in close vicinity.

When they were forced to intermingle with high school students such as when they went over to the gymnasium for physical education, or down to the basement for art and music classes, or down a stairway and through a wide hall that ran beside the auditorium to a commonly shared band room, their movements were as quick and inconspicuous as possible. The cafeteria was another treacherous area. Careful to not make themselves noticeable while waiting in line, seventh-graders grabbed their lunch trays and skulked to one of the back tables where they inhaled lunch and got the heck out of there.

While most were cautious and overwhelmed, there were always a few who were outstandingly bold and headed for the top rung of eventual popularity. Marie was not one of those and neither were Mike Counts nor Madge Schofield, her fellow Valley Falls seventh-graders.

Lockers were another junior high challenge.

It was kind of a mixed bag because on one hand it was pretty cool to mention your locker during casual conversation. On the other hand, you had to memorize a combination, and then there was the business of cramming all of your stuff into that infernally small amount of space and still manage to show up in a designated classroom with the right material before the next bell rang. As with the rest of her fellow seventh-graders, Marie was grateful that there was still homeroom for a full half-day while the second half was spent moving from one classroom to the next.

About two weeks into seventh grade everyone had the system down pat.

Madge's parents went to California in the fall and stayed there until spring so she was only in the Lakeview school system for the beginning and ending of each year. Madge had older brothers and sisters who had already clued her in so she had something of an advantage. At least that's how Marie saw it, plus, Madge's older siblings had already educated Mr. and Mrs. Schofield in how to raise a child.

The Schofields bought Madge a clarinet so that she could take band lessons.

Mike also had the benefit of his older brother John's experience. Mike, however, was an entirely different breed of kid. During junior high Mike was still short for a boy, not really interested in sports or extracurricular activities, but he had one distinct advantage—he was smart! Smart as in the running for valedictorian smart. Science and math came second nature to him and the remainder of his classes ran only slightly behind. Mike appeared not to care one whit about what anyone else thought. So far in *his* education he was in a class by himself.

Marie would have liked to take band lessons and learn how to play the clarinet, or maybe the flute, but Donald and Darlene didn't see it as necessary and she would not be able to stay after school when the band was involved in extra activities. Madge, however, could stay with her married sister who lived in town.

Marie was smart enough but, so far, she lacked the incentive for extra-achievement. An A here and there was fine with her and if the rest were Bs and Cs she was okay with that. No one at home seemed inclined to push her further than that. Marie loved to read and she often sank into a world of make-believe. Even though she envied others to a certain degree, her own world was secure and comfortable.

There was a gradual awakening within Marie that womanhood was approaching but for the time being she preferred not to think about the looming threat of adulthood. One small miracle *had* occurred in the fact that she had ceased to grow and the roundness of childhood was beginning to take on a new shape. She did, however, continue to loathe her straight brown hair and although Mamma used as much patience as she could muster up, Darlene's hair-dressing lessons were a slow and often frustrating work in progress.

Puberty and bras had been a part of Marie's life for over a year and she hated both of them. One day each month was ruined by painful cramps, nausea and diarrhea. Mamma who did not suffer from such female woes didn't seem to understand and Dad thought it was all a bunch of female hooey.

Thank goodness Grandmo's sympathy made up for her parents lack thereof.

Lottie snuggled Marie under a blanket on a sofa that happened to be in the perfect location—in front of warmth radiating from the open door of her living room stove. Lottie wrapped a hot water bottle in a towel and placed it on Marie's tummy. Then she mixed up her aspirin tonic.

Grandmo's aspirin tonic cured almost every kind of ailment that Marie ever suffered.

Lottie used the dull end of a table-knife to pulverize an aspirin into fine granules in the bowl of a teaspoon. She then mixed in a little blackberry wine that she kept stored away for just such purposes on the top shelf of her pantry out on the back porch. She topped off the antidote as she filled a cut-glass whiskey jigger with a little more wine—for a chaser—to make sure the nasty after-taste of the aspirin was thoroughly washed away.

Early one morning Donald, who had no aversion to taking the Lord's name in vain, happened to catch Lottie's monthly doctoring routine.

"Good God, Mom! She'll never grow up if you keep this up!"

Lottie didn't bother to answer or alter her methods. Ever.

Darlene took more of a "whatever works" approach. Her mothering was spread between a thirteen-year-old girl who on some days was going on eighteen and on other days reverted back to an uncooperative five-year-old, an energetic six-year-old boy who was born ready with the ability to drive a tractor and another boy whose babyhood was rapidly growing into toddler stage. If Darlene Simms had ever tended toward hovering over her children, she was losing ground fast.

Donald, the serious young man who came home early from the war to bury himself in ranch work had turned into an outgoing man deeply involved in the affairs of his community. Donald was elected master of the Valley Falls Grange and then he was elected master of Lake County Pomona Grange.

Valley Falls Grange #930 was responsible for drawing out almost everyone who lived in the valley. Folks, who under other circumstances might have been somewhat withdrawn in social and community affairs, were propelled into action by the grange. Aside from the entertainment value of dancing, potlucks, picnics and everything else considered a good time there was the serious business of the national, state and local mission of grange organization.

There were years when the Simms family even managed to attend a few days of the Oregon State Grange's annual convention. Local excitement began to run high when it was announced that the Oregon State Grange would hold its annual convention in Klamath Falls during June of 1955. Lake County granges had agreed to co-sponsor the grand upcoming event, and a flurry of preparation took up most of that spring.

Valley Falls Juvenile Grange held the high-honor of being selected to perform the graduation ceremony when Oregon State Grange juvenile members who had reached a certain age ascended to the subordinate, or adult, level. Elaborate floorwork drills had to be practiced, lines must be memorized and matching formal gowns sewn for the girls. Black dress pants, white shirts and matching ties were purchased for the boys. Practice, practice, practice became the lives of Valley Falls Juvenile Grange youngsters while anxious mothers fussed over every detail.

The subordinate grange Assistant Steward and Lady Assistant Steward were required to participate in the ceremony by leading the grand march into the hall, which in the case of this particular state grange session was the auditorium of Klamath Union High School. Traditionally the part of adult stewards was performed by husband and wife. Donald and Darlene Simms were slated to be the couple. However, by mid-June Darlene would be in her last trimester of pregnancy and it would not be in good taste for an obviously pregnant woman to participate in such a public event.

Donald's cousin, Bernice, marched in Darlene's place.

Klamath Falls, Oregon's heat index rose to over 100 degrees that June afternoon with no air-conditioning at the high school, but nevertheless the Valley Falls Juvenile Grange performed with precision and pride.

When Labor Day weekend rolled around that year Valley Falls Grange sponsored a float in the Round-Up parade to show off the kids. Girls dressed in floor-length, pastel organdy dresses gracefully draped their skirts over the edge of an immaculately cleaned up Simms ranch truck while boys in black pants and white shirts stood with legs braced against sudden stops and starts along the parade route.

Year by year mechanized technology advanced the state of farm equipment, easing the amount of time and manpower necessary to plow fields and harvest crops. There were years when it took some persuasion for Donald to convince his mother that the ranch could do better with a new piece of machinery and yet there were other years when it was Lottie who convinced Donald that they ought to buy a new piece of equipment. The working relationship of the ranch beneath Abert Rim remained amicable between mother and son.

Lottie Simms was generous to Donald and his family. Probably sometimes to the hushed criticism of extended family, neighbors and friends. But Marie could never remember a time when they did not appreciate her grandmother's generosity. They lived comfortable with the knowledge that they, because of her, were more fortunate than many.

Within their family circle Donald was the chief instigator of fun. No one moaned, "I'm bored," or whined, "That's too hard," because Donald refused to listen, but when an opportunity for fun and adventure came along, he was the usual person who promoted the idea.

He made it a point to keep up with the latest news: Farm news, political news, local, state, national and world news. By so doing it was about mid-summer of 1954 when Donald read in the *Oregon Journal* that President Dwight D. Icenhower would dedicate McNary Dam up on the Colombia River. Donald was determined that they should be there.

One noon during the last week of August Donald came in for dinner covered with grain chaff and dust. After he washed up and settled in his place at the end of the table he said, "We'll never be able to give these kids another chance to see a president of the United States. I think we 'd better head up to that dedication."

Darlene felt duty bound to put up some kind of protest, "It's clear into September, the 23rd, we'll have to take Marie out of school again."

He countered, "We take her out almost every fall for a few days to go somewhere or the other. What's a few days of school compared to seeing the president of the United States?"

Lottie put in, "There'll be a terrible crowd. I wonder if we can even find a place to stay."

Donald had it all figured, "We'll get a motel down in Pendleton then we'll get up early and drive on up to the dam."

Marie never forgot the thrill of that day.

The crowd was overwhelming. She felt like her neck was broken as she craned to watch those famous jets, the Blue Angels, fly patterns in a sky that was bluer than blue. Donald maneuvered them into a prime location beside the fish ladder where she was able to snap a picture of President Icenhower with her brand-new Kodak Brownie camera. He rode by in an open convertible just across the fish ladder from where they were standing. She felt a mild amount of concern for the man as she saw how his bald head glistened in the hot September sun.

When the dedication ceremony was over, the crowd was funneled through the interior of the dam so that everyone could be amazed over the power produced by those massive generators. Marie felt like she was drowning in a sea of undulating humanity. Darlene and Lottie navigated the crowd on their own while trying to keep as close as they could. Donald carried Raymond in his arms and instructed Marie to hold on to his suspenders.

Donald was firm as he instructed, "Don't let go, Sister, no matter how many people get between us." And she didn't. She didn't dare.

No one thought about or suggested a vacation that next fall because Sonny was a baby and Mamma thought he was too young to travel. That was the same fall that Hazel Brown Pullen died and it turned out that they traveled anyway, because they went over to Cave Junction for Grandma's funeral.

When they arrived at Grandma's log-cabin house, Lottie stepped in and immediately took charge of Sonny while Donald kept Raymond entertained so that Darlene could participate in the business of helping her sisters and brothers as they sorted and divided Grandma Brown's things. Marie stood back out of the way, but she was mesmerized as she watched them place all of Hazel's beautiful crocheted pieces on her bed. After they were all laid out each of her eight children selected which of those pieces they most wanted.

Grandma made the most beautiful crocheted pieces that Marie had ever seen. Items that you would never imagine being replicated by needle and crochet yarn—Grandma Brown made them.

Marie didn't fully comprehend what she was seeing that day in Grandma Brown's bedroom. It was still hard to remember that Grandma's real last name was Pullen. But Marie was twelve going on thirteen and she was old enough to know that the dividing up process made her feel uneasy. She could tell by the set of her mother's mouth that Mamma didn't like it either.

Marie never understood how it turned out the way it did when Mamma's sisters decided that it was Darlene who should have Grandma's beautiful crocheted table cloth. It was the most gorgeous and intricate piece of Grandma's workmanship.

All of the aunts: Ellen, Mildred, Wilma, Myrtle and Frankie made sure that Darlene understood she had been crowned with a distinct honor. Darlene was given a mandate to take special care of the tablecloth and they declared that the tablecloth was to be was passed from one generation to the next. Marie was aware that she was the generation to follow Mamma, but on that day of Grandma's funeral Marie didn't ponder much over that proclamation.

At twelve, going on thirteen, she couldn't imagine a day when Mamma wouldn't be caring for the tablecloth herself.

That next summer, the summer between Marie's seventh and eighth grades, was a fine summer. The river of life beneath Abert Rim curved into a calm flowing stream that felt like it would flow on the same forever and ever.

# Growing Up Close to Heaven

Grandmo banged the stove lid. It was Marie's signal to get out of bed. She threw back two layers of quilts and made a mad dash from the porch to her bedroom. She snatched up jeans and a shirt and headed for the warmth she knew she would find on the wooden stool tucked behind Grandmo's kitchen stove.

Wooden stools were a dime a dozen at the Simms ranch. Lytle sawed backs off of discarded kitchen chairs. Lottie painted them with high gloss enamel and she even upholstered a few that wound up in the bathroom or bedroom. That particular stool behind the kitchen stove provided both a haven of warmth on chilly summer mornings and cozy contentment when winter winds whipped snow about the eaves of Grandmo's house.

When she was a little girl Marie liked to perch on that stool and listen to her grandmother sing as Lottie busied herself with chores around the kitchen.

Lottie Simms had a warbly soprano voice that was almost good. She sang ballads that were old and long forgotten. She sang about "Two Little Girls in Blue," the sad tale of two sisters in love with two brothers who went off to fight on opposite sides during the Civil War.

Lottie sang another song called, "Little Black Me."

"They always, always pick on me," sang a little Black girl who finally declared, "I'll eat some worms and then I'll die and they'll all be sorry that they picked on me."

Sometimes Marie had a tendency to feel sorry for herself and then she thought about, "Little Black Me."

Now she was older and in fact she was "one of Dad's main buckaroos." That's what Dad called her once and she had become rather puffed up about the whole idea.

When summer temperatures turned hot, she slept out on Lottie's screened-in front porch. After school let out, she could hardly wait for the weather to warm up enough so that she could justify making her move out to the porch. Grandmo had full-custody of her cushioned lounge chair during hot afternoons where she spent hour after hour reading *"Ladies' Home Journal," "McCalls"* and various books from a collection stacked in her bookcase. But when night came Marie pushed the mattress down flat and made up her bed.

Sleeping on that porch was about as close to Heaven as mortal life is ever likely to get. If Marie's happy places were to be listed in the order of their importance, sleeping on Grandmo's front porch would be close to the top of her lifetime list. Soft music of the night lulled her to sleep during a concert played by wisps and whims of the sleeping ranch.

Gentle breezes whispered through leaves of old Poplars and Elms; the creek added its tinkling laughter as it gurgled over rocks and around errant sticks. Dry leaves rustled as nocturnal animals prowled about. Coyotes began their yips here and there and then another would join. Before long a distant pack joined the chorus. The sheep were safe, snugged close to the barn, so coyotes must hunt for their prey elsewhere, among small night-time animals of the sagebrush.

The cold air of breaking dawn on summer mornings always came with a jolt. She always wanted to shrink and snuggle back under the warmth of her covers, but she couldn't. Summer on the ranch came early in the day and often kept working into the coolness of evening.

It was during the mid-1950s that the ranch began to increase its cattle herd by sudden leaps and bounds. Grain fields increased and hay fields increased while the number of sheep remained about the same. Donald and Darlene Simms worked hard to increase the productivity of the ranch.

Lottie was proud of the ranch and, for the most part, content.

Lytle remained a golden memory tucked away in a secret place where Lottie often chose to retreat. He spoke to her soul while he convinced her that life is meant to be lived and enjoyed. He often reminded her that her work was not done. He talked to her about Donald, of Darlene and of three healthy, happy, vibrant grandchildren.

As his memory whispered in her ear, she remembered his caresses and then his soul would stroke her soul. And while she was there, in that sacred place, he managed to convince her that life *is* good, that together their legacy would live on for those left behind as their descendants took their own views of God's Country.

For several years Donald declared that pasture beneath the rim was not sufficient to summer their increasing number of cattle. When Lottie questioned him, he said, "Well we're gonna have to build fence over on Dicks Creek. Sheep don't need fences when there's a sheepherder, but now we're running cattle."

Springtime became fence building time.

Donald drove on ahead with bundles of iron posts, rolls of barbed wire and other fence building supplies thrown in the bed of the old Jeep pickup. The rest of them followed in the Jeep station wagon loaded down with lunch, blankets, thermoses of coffee and canteens of water. Donald easily convinced his wife and his kids that they were having a fun weekend adventure.

There were other years when fence building went into higher, rougher country and then Donald hired Mike Counts on weekends. He and Mike packed supplies on a horse as they made the rugged steep climb from Dicks Creek to Mill Lake.

Ordinarily he used a different horse but for some reason one Saturday morning Donald decided to use his saddle horse, Cotton-eye. As they strung the wire Cotton-eye caught his front left leg in a piece of tangled wire. Donald tried to lead Cotton-eye out of the tangle, but the horse spooked and began to crow hop and buck. Tension tightened the wire as the barbs slashed deep into Cotton-eye's left foreleg and ripped into his flesh leaving a huge gash through his artery.

Blood squirted and gushed as Donald, frantic, remembered the piece of leather he used to tie up the reins. His hands and fingers felt clumsy as he tried to work fast while he ripped the leather from the reins and then reached down and around his horse's quivering leg as he worked to tie a tourniquet.

Finally, it was tight enough. The gushing stopped. Without speaking he and Mike turned and began to maneuver Cotton-eye ever so slowly down the mountain. Together they held up the front of the crippled horse as best they could. It was maddingly slow as they eased him over downed tree limbs and picked a path around boulders.

Finally, they came to the truck. Donald had left it backed it into a dirt bank where they unloaded Cotton-eye that morning. Mike tugged to help Cotton-eye raise each leg while Donald urged him from the front and thus, they managed to load the horse. Carefully, slowly Donald eased the old International down the rutted, rocky road. When he finally reached the highway, he headed toward Lakeview and the vet's clinic pushing the truck as fast as it would go.

In the end they managed to save Cotton-eye. Mike, it turned out later, went through Oregon State University and on to veterinary school.

This June morning, in the cold grey light of breaking dawn Donald and everyone else were in fine spirits. Today was the annual cattle drive when they moved the cattle across to summer pasture up on Dicks Creek.

Marie had worked with her father yesterday, as they gathered cattle from under the rim and so had Raymond because now, he too was old enough to ride and gather cattle. As cows and calves, some in a bunch here and then another bunch coming later, streamed down from the Rehart Trail and from out north, through the Indian Trail, the three of them pushed cattle into a small field above the barn where they could easily be regathered in the morning.

Loyd rode up early, before the sun peeked over the rim, to help gather. Before they pushed the cattle into the big corral, Dow Frakes and Coop were out from town and unloading their horses. Ed Deboy was right behind and on his horse in a jiffy.

By the time sunbeams were streaming through the heavy low-laying morning dust, the cattle had left the corral. Cows bunched, ducked and dodged as they crowded through the wide wooden gate, all the while searching and bawling for this spring's calves.

Darlene kept hold, as best she could, on Sonny while he teetered and swayed back and forth on the top board of the corral fence. He was excited too, and he was yearning to be on a horse and part of the crowd. She and Lottie waited and watched the gradually disappearing herd as they trailed south toward the timber-culture.

Donald took the point. He gave Cotton-eye his head as they worked some of the older cows out toward the front. With any luck the others would fall in, settle down and they'd soon be strung out. Dow, Coop and Ed rode the sides and pushed wandering strays back toward the herd. Loyd kept an eye on the rear where Raymond, Marie and Patty pushed from behind.

The cattle-drive held an extra excitement for Marie this morning because Patty Nichols came along with Loyd. Patty was Marie's cousin from down in San Bruno, California—in the bay area of San Francisco. Because Patty was a city girl Marie felt somewhat inclined to show off her expert cowgirl ways.

Patty was visiting at Aunt Leona's and Loyd's place down on Crooked Creek with her Grandmother, Elva, who was Aunt Leona's daughter, making Patty Aunt Leona's great-granddaughter. Elva made an extended visit each summer to spend time with her mother and it was during those visits that Marie and Patty became lifelong soulmates.

This morning Loyd saddled his old bay mare, Lady, for Patty's excursion into the world of cattle-drives.

They pushed the cattle across a small piece of Forest Service land before they began to cross a wide expanse called the Eades Field.

Lottie often talked about the Eades Field. She talked about a time back in the old days when the massive field located just over the bluff which borders the east side of Crooked Crook still belonged to her father, Sol Chandler. There was a slight bitter edge to her voice as she talked about how it was that her brothers, Roy and George had lost it to the bank.

That first year when they crossed the Eades Field Marie was interested to finally see the entire length of it. They drove the cattle beside a small mineral seep known as Soda Springs, but Loyd called it "Sody Springs."

Nearing the south end of the field they had to push the cattle through a wire gate and on to right-of-way beside highway 395 where Crooked Creek streams by. As they approached the gate, they passed crumbling remains of an old sheep shearing barn and corrals. Marie remembered when she was a little girl and her mother placed her high on a platform where she watched as the lambs were sorted out to be shipped from those corrals. And then they saw scattered pieces left from an old sawmill that stood over on the banks of Moss Creek.

As they passed the corrals, Donald pushed Cotton-eye on out front and hurried ahead to open the gate.

The cattle funneled through the gate and immediately slowed as they began to wade into deep, thick grass growing beside Crooked Creek. Dow and Ed kept the cows pushed away from the highway for as long as they could, but there was about three-quarters to a full mile stretch where they were forced to move directly on the pavement.

That part of the cattle-drive was a little scary and a little fun all at the same time. Marie felt self-conscious, like she was on some kind of display, when tourists hollered, waved and took pictures.

Donald's horse, Cottoneye, loved the attention! He arched his neck, pranced and chewed his bit. He was a good looker and he knew it.

Donald bought Cotton-eye from a man up in Paisley who had trained the horse well. As long as there was a rider Cottoneye was all business, one of the best cow-horses around. But there was a problem, well perhaps not so much a problem as there was a ridiculously fun side of Cottoneye in the fact that when he was not being ridden, he became a spoiled pet.

Donald usually took an extra sandwich along for Cottoneye. While ground-tied he lowered his head and with big, sorrowful horse eyes he begged for scraps of food. Cottoneye loved people food.

One day Raymond, who was hungry as all get out after a long day of gathering cows, raced to the house to make himself a sandwich. As he returned to help with the sort, he climbed over the corral fence. Donald yelled across to Raymond, "Bring Cotton-eye over here."

Raymond, following his father's orders, led the horse through milling cows. Cotton-eye eyed the sandwich, stretched over Raymond's shoulder and snagged it out of his hand.

Raymond was so mad at Cotton-eye that he got red in the face and proceeded to tell the blasted horse off. Everyone else saw what happened and doubled over laughing and that made Raymond even madder!

As the front of the herd approached Bean's Corner Donald turned the cows up Dick's Creek road while Dow and Coop rode into the turn making sure that none of them strayed on down the highway. The rest of the trip was easy going except for when the drovers were forced to eat powder fine dust as the herd moved up Chalk Hill. Gaining the top, the old cows streamed eagerly down into the canyon where Dicks Creek runs its course and other cows followed quickly behind.

Before the cattle and their drovers had gone out of sight that morning, Darlene left the corral and hurried back to the house where she began to pack food into pasteboard boxes. She and Lottie loaded everything into Dad's jeep station wagon. Lottie, Darlene and Sonny were already there and waiting when the cows headed downhill to green grass and water. As soon as the last cow streamed by, they unloaded coffee, water and food for hungry and thirsty cowhands.

There was never, ever, anywhere, anytime in Marie's life when food tasted better than those sumptuous work-party picnics that Darlene spread on a clean cloth under juniper and pine trees up on Dicks Creek.

Marie loved work at the ranch, especially if it involved some kind of cowgirl work. When she was in high school, however, she began to envy her town friends because they had summer jobs with a paycheck. She would like to have a paycheck. But when she whined about it, Dad reminded her that she had a job at the ranch and she had a sheep and two cows.

With a lot of help from both her grandfather and her mother Marie had raised Mary from a bummer lamb. Molly, her cow that Marie helped Grandpo raise as an orphan, was quite prolific as she added to Marie's bank account. A few years ago, Dad let her buy a registered Polled Hereford heifer she named Goldie. Between Molly's calves and Goldie's offspring her college account was adding up.

Her mother needed help in the kitchen. There were fruits and vegetables to be picked, there was firewood to be corded and stacked in the woodshed, livestock had to be fed and watered. If it rained on bales of hay still in the field they had to be turned, sheep had to be kept out of the alfalfa and brought close to the barn at night to protect them from cayotes and best of all, as far as Marie was concerned, cattle had to be gathered, sorted, branded and moved.

Furthermore, Marie was expected to learn the so-called feminine skills, and it was nice happenstance that Marie had some talent for cooking and sewing.

Marie and Madge began 4-H sewing classes just as soon as they were old enough. In the beginning Madge's mother, Mrs. Schofield, taught them, but when they began advanced lessons Genevieve Elder, who lived across the valley at the Elder Ranch, took over. Genevieve knew everything there was to know about the latest sewing methods.

Marie was expected to enroll in high school Home Economics. It was alright with her. She was expected to make straight A's in Home

Ec and she did. Between 4-H sewing and high school Home Ec her wardrobe began to bulge. Lottie was generous and if Marie desired a certain piece of material Grandmo usually bought it. That first winter of Marie's high school Donald did some remodeling over in Lottie's house to enlarge Marie's closet.

Lottie made sure that her granddaughter owned a few of the latest Jantzen, White Stag or Pendleton sweaters and woolen skirts purchased from either the Mary Jo shop in Lakeview or from La Pointes over in Klamath Falls. In spite of Donald's remodeling project Marie's wardrobe spilled over to take up a full one-half of Lottie's own closet.

It was probably a wise decision on destiny's part that Marie's bedroom wound up across the road in her grandmother's house.

There were two high schools in Lake County: Lakeview High and Paisley High. Students from North Lake County had to board out as they attended either Paisley, Lakeview or possibly LaPine or Bend High Schools. Most of them came to Lakeview. Students from the California state line community of New Pine Creek were bused up to Lakeview for High School as were West Side and Thomas Creek students. Incoming Lakeview High School freshman classes burst at the seams and everyone's friendship circle grew by nearly one-half again.

Small as Lakeview High School was it was considered urban by Lake County standards.

When Valley Falls kids entered Lakeview High School, they were self-confident. Most rural children of post-war Lake County were fortunate enough to have been raised by solid families who were in support of decisions made by those in charge of their education. They came from parents who took the necessary time required to reinvent themselves as 4-H Club leaders. Those parents gave their children Saturday nights at the grange hall. Some of that was quite by accident, of course, because as the parents spent those weekend nights dancing with generous potluck midnight suppers, they were giving their children a core foundation of social skills that propelled them easily into the rest of their lives.

# The Grand Tour

Dinner dishes were washed, dried, put away and the kitchen cleaned up after Dad and John Counts went back to the hay field. It was so darned hot that Marie could easily beg off from work out in the woodpile where slabs had to be corded and blocks thrown into the woodshed. She hated that nasty job.

Lottie's front porch provided a protected and lazy retreat on warm summer afternoons. During the winter a row of tall windows were set with glass panes, but when the weather warmed up those glass windows were removed so that air flowed and circulated while screens kept the flies and mosquitos outside.

Lottie relaxed on her lounge chair with her face hidden behind July's edition of the *Oregon State Grange Bulletin*.

"That'd sure be a nice trip."

Marie looked up, "What trip's that, Grandmo?"

She was deep in another Zane Grey novel. Last summer Marie had discovered the old-west stories of Zane Grey.

Zane Grey novels were stacked in several bookcases tucked into various nooks and crannies of both Lottie's house and Donald's and Darlene's house. Marie grabbed every opportunity she could find to bury her nose in one of those books. She couldn't get enough of Grey's accounting of handsome cowboys who overthrew lawless and corrupt evil doers on the wide-open spaces of the western frontier.

Her imagination easily conjured up images of those magnificent horses that Zane Grey artfully brought to life. There was always a beautiful heroine and although he never came right out and said so, the heroine was often a bit naïve. On the books' final pages, the daring, handsome and carefree cowboy hero won the young woman's heart. Untold, but surmised was the fact that they lived forever in blissful peace on a beautiful ranch overlooking a sage-covered valley below.

"The Oregon State Grange is sponsoring a bus traveling back east to Grand Rapids, Michigan for the National Grange Convention. They'll be traveling clear across to Washington D. C., Philadelphia, New York City, on up to Toronto, Canada, Niagara Falls and then circle back to Grand Rapids for the convention."

"Wow! You ought to go, Grandmo, and *I* could go along with you."

"I'm sure you'd like that, but I'm afraid you can't," she laughed.

"They'll be leaving the end of October and the tour won't return home until just before Thanksgiving. We'd be gone for a whole month and you, my dear, will be in school."

"I could make it up—it would be easy."

"I don't think so. You'll be a sophomore and you're going to be taking some very important classes. At least you should be. You ought to take typing and you'd better think about enrolling in business classes like bookkeeping and business math."

If Lottie Simms had any influence over her granddaughter's education, she was determined that Marie would take what were in Lottie's opinion useful classes so that she was equipped to make a living for herself—just in case she had to. Lottie saw no future in Marie's fanciful ideas about traveling the world writing for publications such as *Life Magazine* or *National Geographic*. Those ideas, Lottie thought, were romantic notions not meant for down-to-earth country girls who ought to marry some nice boy, settle down to raise children and keep a good house.

Those business classes were easy for Marie and she didn't mind taking them. Doing so kept Grandmo happy.

In Marie's fifteen-year-old opinion she could easily make up any lost time. "Oh Grandmo, I could make it up. I could take books along and study at night."

"Oh sure." Lottie dismissed the subject as she folded the paper, laid it down and picked up the *Oregon Journal.*

Marie picked up the Bulletin to read about the trip for herself. What an adventure! Traveling on a chartered Trailways bus, staying in nice hotels in interesting cities while they drove across the entire mid-section of the United States. Four days were scheduled for Washington D. C. and another four days were scheduled in New York City. Three days were planned in Grand Rapids for the National Grange convention and then back across the Midwest, Wyoming and Idaho.

She didn't intend to let Grandmo forget about the educational aspect of a trip like that.

In spite of her practical, down-to-earth, common-sense nature, wheels of imagination began to spin in Lottie's own head. She mused, more than she supposed she ought to, about the idea of traveling to places she had always wanted to see. It *was* a good opportunity. She could give Marie an educational advantage in history alone, not to mention seeing places she might never have the opportunity to visit again. When she mentioned the trip to Donald and Darlene, they were so blindsided they hardly knew what to say.

After she left and went back across the road to her own house Donald said to Darlene, "I didn't think Mom had that much get-up-and-go left in her."

"Neither did I," replied Darlene.

"A month out of school for Marie! I don't know what to say."

Lottie mentioned the trip to her sisters. She figured they'd think she was being outlandish and spending her money foolishly. When she had bought the Kaiser Manhattan, she accidently overheard Lora exclaim to Gladys, "Do you know how much she paid for that car? It was over $3,000.00!"

But to her surprise May, Lora and Gladys said that she ought to go ahead and take the trip. When Lottie mentioned it to friends and neighbors up and down the valley, *they* said that she ought to do it.

As a matter of fact, whenever she confessed her notion to others, especially older folks, they said, "Oh, for heaven's sake, don't worry about Marie missing school. She's a smart girl; she'll figure it out. Look at the educational value for her—she'd never get that much in two or three years of school. Imagine the historical sites she'll see! It's a fabulous opportunity you'd be giving her."

When the August bulletin arrived and there was still space available Lottie went ahead and sent in reservations for two.

Marie was thrilled. She couldn't believe it was actually going to happen.

However, and it was a huge however, she was told over and over, again and again, that the only, *only*, way she would be allowed to go was that her grades would have to be straight A's. Well, nothing less than B+. If they weren't—Grandmo would just have to cancel. That's all there was to it.

It's fair to say that when school began Lottie, who was almost as worried about Marie's grades as Marie was, hounded her over homework every night. Marie applied herself as she never had before.

Darlene made an appointment with Mr. Mulholland who was the principal of Lakeview High School and even *he* said that it was a fabulous opportunity. Some of the teachers were astonished, but they agreed to provide books and homework assignments.

A trip was scheduled to Klamath Falls so that Lottie could update her luggage to Samsonite. A month's worth of travel clothes had to be considered. For days Darlene and Lottie put their heads together discussing the matter.

They came to mutual consent that skirts and sweaters could be mixed and matched. Underwear and nighties could be rinsed out in the evening. She should have a generous supply of nylon stockings on hand. Marie ought to have at least one dress-up outfit and a pair of low-heeled black pumps. She needed a new pair of substantial flats for everyday and walking tours. Mid-length car coats were the latest craze so one of those would do nicely.

Hustle and bustle were the order of each day. There was no time to waste.

Finally, Lottie had a detailed itinerary in hand plus an extra copy to leave with Donald and Darlene. She had plenty of cash and a good supply of travel checks. Marie packed her schoolwork assignments and on the morning of departure everything came together. Her new clothes were neatly packed into shiny, unblemished luggage and Dad's 8.mm movie camera plus extra film were safely tucked into a carry-on bag.

An old familiar knot tightened in Marie's stomach that October morning as Dad drove Grandmo's car away from the ranch. Everyone was in a happy mood, but as they passed familiar landmarks Marie's knot grew heavier. At the store Donald made a right turn onto Highway 395. Abert Lake glistened under the polish of early morning sun. They left the lake behind as they passed over the ridge where the hogback road takes off toward Plush and then they crossed the desert to Burns. After Burns the countryside grew less familiar.

Nerves began to pick away at both Lottie and Marie as Donald drove into the bus depot's parking lot at Ontario, over on the Oregon/Idaho border. The tour left Portland that morning but they, along with Jack Moffit and his wife and John and Katy Dick from down in New Pine Creek, had made arrangements to join the tour in Ontario. The bus drove in as soon as they arrived and before they knew it everything was loaded and ready for departure.

They hugged Mom, Dad, Raymond and Sonny, kissed them goodbye and boarded the bus. There was a moment of near despair when Marie realized that she would not see them again for a month, but she sucked in a deep breath and surged forward. A month can be a long time.

Homesickness was a familiar agony for Marie. To anticipate adventure was one thing, but when it came down to leaving her family, she could hardly stand it. There was one summer when she spent a week at a camp for grange kids and before two days had passed, she decided that she would never do that again. Occasionally she spent a weekend or stayed overnight with school friends and that was almost too long. She loved it when friends stayed over with her at the ranch, but the reverse was too hard.

As the bus drove away, her parents and little brothers waved and Lottie and Marie waved back. Marie swallowed hard so that no tattletale tears would ooze out and trickle down her cheeks.

By the following morning as the bus drove away from the hotel in Boise, Idaho Marie and Lottie were in fine spirits and well on their way.

Marie was the only young person and for the first day her youth was an unforeseen novelty to her fellow passengers. Her manners were good however, she had been raised that way, and she had been taught to appreciate opportunities. By the end of that trip, Marie had temporarily acquired a whole passel of honorary aunts and uncles.

The trip was a blast.

Every morning they got an early start. About three or four o'clock in the afternoon they pulled up beside another outstanding hotel in another city or sometimes it was a town of special interest.

One of those towns was Dodge City, Kansas. No official tour was planned but they were able to persuade the local curators to open up Boot Hill for the evening. It was a fun night and what a group they were! A bunch of well-heeled happy-go-lucky grandmas and grandpas touring an outrageous Halloween cemetery and Marie was along for the ride!

If nothing had been scheduled for the evening Lottie and Marie explored close to the hotel. After dinner they returned to their room where Marie did homework while Lottie wrote postcards to everyone back home.

They spent one night at the Mark Twain Hotel in St. Louis, Missouri.

Lottie had written ahead to Lillie Mae about their overnight stay in St. Louis. Lillie Mae was the daughter of Lytle's brother, Tom. Tom's wife, Aunt Nellie, had died several years before and Lottie often expressed her regret that she had not been able to visit with Nellie one more time.

Gene, Lillie Mae's brother, was already there and waiting for them when the bus arrived at the hotel. He drove Lottie and Marie out to Lillie Mae's home for dinner, and when they arrived, they found Uncle Tom waiting for them. Tom and Lottie were the last of that Simms generation. Although they were unaware of it, that evening was the last time that the Lytle Simms family was ever together with the Tom Simms family. It was the end of an era.

Marie felt something that night that she had never felt before—nor ever afterward. The sensation overwhelmed her to such a degree that she never mentioned it to her grandmother or ever asked her grandmother how she felt that night. That evening in the presence of Tom Simms felt like she was seeing and hearing her grandfather again. The one looked so much like the other and the tones and inflections in their voices were so much alike that when her uncle spoke it sounded like her grandfather's voice. Something about it made her want to grasp the sensation and keep it in her heart forever.

The rolling hills of West Virginia were beautifully dressed in their fall colors. The group on the bus anticipated Washington D.C. with every picture postcard scene that swept by the bus. They saw everything in Washington D.C. that could be squeezed into four days. They spent one day at Mount Vernon and it was glorious. The days were long but they never tired as they drank in great moments of history. It was like a dream for Marie.

They stopped over in Philadelphia to visit Independence Hall and the Betsy Ross House. It was awe inspiring to be in such a historic place where the footsteps of our nation's forefathers once tread. It came as a jolt, however, to discover that such a sacred place was located in the heart of a disgusting city slum. Years later, when Marie read that the area surrounding Independence Hall had been cleaned up and turned into a designated national historic location, both she and her grandmother were greatly relieved.

The bus rolled along on a slightly elevated highway and as they traveled, they rode in silence. They gazed upon block after endless block of filthy, ragged slums—they, traveling on the bus who were such healthy well-kept individuals. How could it be that fellow humans were reduced to live in such a condition? To rural Oregonians who had lived their lives in the fresh air and pastoral settings up and down the Willamette Valley it felt like a disgrace to mankind. Lottie and Marie were dumbfounded. Those Eastern Oregon travelers who loved the big wide-open of desert rangeland and forests of Ponderosa Pine had never witnessed people living in such a state of despair.

Although Marie loved the idea of being in New York City she did not care much for the city. To a ranch girl of Eastern Oregon those deep walls of concrete and steel reminded her of being in a box canyon. It felt like she could not get a good breath. She enjoyed the fresh sea breeze when they took a ferry to Liberty Island, and there she climbed the long spiral steps inside the statue to get a good look out of Lady Liberty's crown. Another day they boarded a ferry that took them around Manhattan Island. An aircraft carrier, the Independence, was moored in the harbor. The massive bulk of that ship was something she had never imagined.

One day they were taken on a tour of China Town and a mission district. Once again, Marie was disgusted by filth. They walked around people prone on the sidewalks—were they dead? Were they drunk? Were they sleeping? Their guide seemed to be totally indifferent. There was a missionary in every little church they entered who told them how bad off the folks were and begged for money. Perhaps they were hard-hearted, or perhaps they were tight fisted, but those rural Oregonians who had toiled from day dawn to the first light of evening for their farms and their daily bread could not understand why those people did not sober up and clean up so that they could find a job and take care of themselves.

Marie found the open-air markets in China Town appalling. Dad knew better than to hang fresh butchered meat out in the open air with no protection from flies. Marie remembered how Dad always pulled a clean wool sack over a deer's carcass and pulled the carcass up high so that nothing could touch it. It took several years after for Marie, just like her father, to tolerate Chinese food. There came a day, however, when Marie was forced to discover that Chinese food is fantastic.

There were, of course, wonderful things to see and do in New York City—Marie had to admit that. One evening she was in the audience for a live television game show. She marveled at the view from the top of the Empire State Building. Their hotel was located one block from the famous Macy's Department Store and Lottie and Marie shopped. Grandmo let Marie buy a beautiful royal blue sweater and a silver-plated chunky necklace that had a triangular shaped crest on one side and a mirror on the other. For the length of about one-week after she returned to school, Marie was the envy of all her girly classmates.

Everyone on the tour admitted to a certain amount of relief when they left the city and began to drive through magical fall colors. Vermont was breathtaking. After they left Toronto the bus traveled back to Niagara Falls. What a powerful site. Lottie acted like she wasn't one bit worried when she let Marie ride a cable car across the boiling, churning rapids below the falls.

In Grand Rapids the National Grange Convention was an extravaganza to top all extravaganzas. What an idea—there was even an underground tunnel to connect the hotel with the convention center! And right there in the hotel lobby was a prize-winning steer comfortably penned, continuously fed and nicely cleaned up at frequent intervals. She couldn't wait to tell Dad about that one!

When they arrived in Grand Rapids it turned out that someone who was someone in the National Grange discovered that a fifteen-year-old girl from rural Oregon had arrived on a tour bus. Before she knew what happened to her Marie was recruited to be on a youth drill team who opened and closed a special evening session of the National

Grange. She was scared to death, but at the same time she was grateful that her mother persisted and packed a dress-up outfit—just in case!

Everyone on the tour, especially Grandmo, was proud of her and although her knees quaked through the entire event, she guessed that no one noticed how nervous she was. Afterward, there was a picture taking ceremony and sure enough a picture appeared in the National Grange's monthly magazine. The fame of her picture in that magazine lasted for one entire Valley Falls Grange meeting.

When the bus pulled away from Grand Rapids Marie couldn't wait to get home. There was a long letter from home waiting when they arrived in New York City and another when they arrived in Grand Rapids. Marie devoured those letters. Dad wrote some. Mom wrote some and even Raymond added a scribbly line from him and Sonny. Those letters were so wonderful to Marie that she vowed she would never be mad at anyone in her family ever again and that didn't last overly long either.

They spent one exciting night in Davenport, Iowa. Not the place you would expect a lot of excitement; however they wound up spending most of the night in the hotel lobby because of a tornado watch. It turned out that the tornado touched down across the Mississippi River in Rock Island, Illinois, and that was as close to a tornado as Marie ever wanted to get.

The last night out was spent at a fancy new Thunderbird Motel in Boise, Idaho. They ordered a special Thanksgiving dinner for their last evening together. Everyone proclaimed what a wonderful experience the entire adventure had been. Everyone vowed that they would always stay in touch and for many years after that grand trip Lottie sent and received Christmas cards and letters from their fellow travel companions.

As the bus approached the depot in Ontario Marie's heart began to race. And then she saw them. There they were—Dad was grinning from ear to ear. Mom waved and smiled her welcome mother's smile. Raymond grinned as he waved and Sonny was jumping up and down—his freckles shining and his straight red hair bouncing up and down like a rubber ball.

# At Home in God's Country

If Marie could always live as a country girl who rode the Valley Falls bus to Lakeview High School life wouldn't be half bad. Her home at the ranch beneath Abert Rim was comfortable and happy. Donald and Darlene were lively, good-looking young parents who loved each other, their children and occasionally, to the best of their ability, indulged them somewhat. Her younger brothers, Raymond and Sonny, were bright, they were cute, they were full of the dickens and quite often a mess. Her grandmother, Lottie, spoiled all of them and Marie had as much and sometimes more than many of her friends.

Valley Falls Grange #930 and the Valley Falls Grange Women's Home Economics club (better known as the Home Ec Club) were the social center of the valley. Ladies of the Home Ec Club hosted their auxiliary meetings in proper style. Dainty desserts were served on fashionable glass plates with delicate cups of coffee, tea or punch along with pastel paper nut cups filled with mints and assorted nuts. Paper napkins with delicate floral prints accompanied the plates as they were passed around.

Although adults of the valley still resisted the idea of their kids entering 4-H and FFA livestock in the county fair, they pulled together to provide interesting 4-H projects beyond the usual sewing and gardening with projects such as leather work, camp cookery and a horseback riding club. Donald Simms and Doug Elder did break over one year as they trucked horses to town so that the Valley Falls 4-H horseback club could participate in the Labor Day parade. Neither the horses nor the riders were all that thrilled with the end result and so it never happened again.

It was Marie's opinion that high school was fabulous.

It slipped up, to a certain degree, on Donald and Darlene when Marie began to talk about going to college. And then they thought that Raymond and Sonny might want to attend college, also.

Another decade had turned—it was 1960. There was peace and prosperity. The technology of modern machinery plus scientific approaches to farming and raising livestock were the agricultural news of the day.

Parents of Marie's town friends were mill workers, store clerks, mechanics and small business owners. Some of their fathers had been teenage boys when they left high school to fight in the war. Often their mothers were girls who had rushed into marriage and babies so that boys would leave a posterity just in case they didn't return from the war. Now those parents wanted more and better for their children and a college education was expected for many of Marie's classmates and friends.

Marie's goal was to maintain a grade point average that would be accepted on a college application. Slightly beneath that goal she desired that her closet be adequately filled with the latest clothing trend. She spent a considerable amount of energy as she attempted to achieve the latest hairdo by rolling her hair every night and still get a decent night's sleep in those prickly brush rollers. Fun times with friends were very important, and catching the attention of cute boys was another consideration.

Darlene slid into her role as mother of a teenage daughter. It was a comfortable transition because she tended to take things as they came, from one day to the next. Like all mothers of all time, she wanted the best for her children. She was, however, faced with future ideas that were completely foreign to her.

For that matter, up until the last couple of years Donald, himself, had not given much thought to Marie's future. The boys, he figured, would grow up someday way off in the future and take over the ranch. He also supposed it would be convenient if an upstanding young man on a ranch located in the near vicinity would take a shine to Marie. So far it didn't look like the part about Marie was going to happen and it was way too soon to worry about the boys.

When Darlene Brown fell in love with Donald and began to make her home at the ranch, she fell in love with more than Donald. She fell in love with the ranch. She had never expected to live such a bountiful life in such a beautiful place.

When Darlene grew up in South Dakota and Nebraska as the middle daughter of a farmer who worked for others during the dust bowl and depression, survival had been her utmost concern. Moving year after year from one location to another where work might be more plentiful, Darlene had never allowed herself to grow overly attached to material possessions.

Darlene was as rooted to the ranch beneath the rim as the old Poplar trees that lined the ditch bank in front of their house. There were days when she almost forgot that she had ever lived in any other place.

She reveled in birthdays and Christmas. To be able to buy presents for her children, Christmas decorations and ornaments for the tree, to clothe her children without worry and the availability of all the ingredients needed to bake and cook wonderful meals for her family were all wonderful to Darlene. It was such a miracle to her that she never became able to stray far from her cautious nature as she selected and purchased her wares, but Darlene's children always profited from her generous loving nature.

There had been an evening when Darlene found herself dressed in her own best clothes as she straightened and smoothed Marie's formal gown, trying to calm the nerves of her thirteen-year-old-daughter while Marie waited in the anteroom to be initiated into Job's Daughters. Darlene was the calming influence because Marie was scared. Lottie, however, had been over the moon thrilled that her granddaughter had been asked to join such a prestigious social group for young ladies.

Marie did not like Job's Daughters. She never got used to it.

Darlene gently encouraged Marie to attend the meetings. She took pains to look after her white robe with its royal purple cord. Marie *tried* to like Job's Daughters, but she was never able to see the profit of such an organization and gradually she became inactive. Marie knew that she had her mother's support. She also knew that her father was secretly glad when he no longer had to chauffeur Marie in to town on snowy winter nights to go to a meeting that Marie didn't want to attend.

For the most part, Lottie kept her mouth shut.

Eventually Marie came to a point where she realized that it was nice for her to learn how to conduct herself in more refined social settings. At the time, however, she compared the sweet floor work marches that the pianist tinkled away on a modern spinet piano to the floor work marches done at the grange. When Aunt Lora Newton's hands came down on piano keys everyone stepped in time as they marched to rousing renditions of "Anchors Away" or "Stars and Stripes Forever."

When Lora Chandler Boone Newton ascended the rough wooden platform down at the grange hall and laid her plump hands on the old upright's black and whites, vibrant music burst forth. As she struck up The Star-Spangled Banner you could hear the drum roll of the United States Navy Band. Everyone straightened their shoulders and stood tall, be they old or young, folks put their hands over their hearts and sang out with their fullest ability.

No sir, there no wishy-washing or denying of patriotism down at the Valley Falls Grange, nor was there any doubt that God in his Heaven was in charge of it all.

On the other hand, Marie loved the social side of advanced Home Economics classes. She loved the teas and style revues. Darlene loved them with her and showed up for every event dressed-up in her nicest with her thick beautiful hair and the barest trace of makeup. Marie might have been a ranch girl from Valley Falls but she had one teeniest, tiniest edge over some of her classmates: Her mother was one of the youngest. She being the first born of a girl who married right out of high school.

Marie loved and envied her mother's beautiful hair. It was thick, with a deep rich color. Darlene knew how to neatly twist her hair into stylish French knots. They were so simple and yet, in Marie's opinion, they were far more attractive than those of women who spent more time on themselves. She was quiet and demure among the crowd of mothers. She was not bossy or pushy. She smiled in pride as she watched her children perform. And for all that, she was one of a kind.

Darlene Simms accomplished a lot. In fact, there came a day when she broke a glass ceiling for the women of Valley Falls when without asking or expecting such an outrageous notion, she was elected Master of the Valley Falls Grange.

There was a part of Darlene that wanted to decline the whole honor, but she squared her shoulders and with quiet dignity she upheld her place among former patriarchs of the grange. She had previously served her time as Chairwoman of the Home Ec Club; she knew what to do and she did it.

The advances of time changed almost everything in the valley.

Vest Carroll retired from driving the school bus and Ed Gunkel took over. The transition was not easy as Ed's red hair was an indication of his red-hot temper, particularly when it came to the boys who had his number from the first day. It took a couple of years for Ed and the school superintendent to figure out that he was a better fit working for the Oregon State Highway Department.

After Ed resigned Dick Stubbs took over as Valley Falls school bus driver. Dick was a young man who knew how to handle the kids and within a couple of days he had the full respect of the boys. He was a good-looking young man and the high school girls liked him almost to the point of a crush.

It came as a shock when Vest and Bessie Carroll retired from the Valley Falls Store to follow their son, Herbert, and his family up to La Grande in the northeastern corner of Oregon. No one could imagine the store without Vest and Bessie. But the transition turned out to be smooth when Bessie's brother, George Cormie, and his wife, Rose, took over the store. Life in the valley went on although Lottie Simms and Bessie Carroll who were the best of best friends never completely got over the grief of that parting.

One year while they wintered in California, Jake Schofield died. After that Mrs. Schofield and Madge spent less and less time in Valley Falls. Mrs. Schofield put their farm land into the soil bank program of the federal government. By the end of the 1950s it turned out that so much grain was being grown in the United States that there was now a surplus so government programs like the soil bank kicked in to ease the market.

Madge spent her last year of high school in California. Madge and Marie always remained friends with the kind of bond that is sometimes shared by two kindred spirits. Marie had grown into a more confident person and although she missed Madge terribly, she mustered on with little to no trouble.

The women's organization of the Oregon State Grange sponsored sewing and cooking contests and the ladies of Valley Falls Grange eagerly joined the competition. One year Pat Weekly went so far as to win the state championship in a baking contest and her prize was a brand-new cook stove.

Darlene entered both the baking and sewing contests and although she never advanced to the state level, she won district events in both of those categories.

Late one Friday morning of a blustery April day Donald had the chores done and he had Sonny in tow as he came through Lottie's back door. He picked up the coffee pot from the back of her kitchen stove and poured himself a cup of coffee while Sonny settled down with Marie's old toy Farmall tractor on the front room rug. Lottie put down a letter she was writing and asked, "What are you two up to?"

Donald grunted his reply, "Darlene's baking another one of them Pineapple Chiffon cakes for the Pomona grange contest out at Westside tomorrow."

"Oh."

Lottie didn't need any further explanation. That particular Pineapple Chiffon cake had gained its own reputation as it proceeded to win at various levels of the Oregon State Grange baking contest. Every member of the Simms family knew they 'd better stay out of Darlene's kitchen when baking was in progress. In fact, when the cake was at last beaten out at a district level, Darlene never baked it again and no one in the family cared that she didn't.

Darlene's dinner tables were a masterpiece of abundance. During the winter, except for holiday celebrations, things slacked off somewhat, but as soon as spring arrived there was a continual arrival of dinner-time extras what with lambs being docked, sheep shearing, branding, cattle drives, one of the Counts boys during haying season, extra help bucking bales on the weekend, grain harvesting, hunting season and on through the fall. And that did not account for the steady stream of Sunday company.

Darlene planned a big Sunday dinner because folks were bound to show up from town: Aunt Lora and Uncle Harry Newton, the cousins or maybe Ed and Happy DeBoy for a game of pinochle. The list was endless. Darlene Simms never wanted anyone to leave her house unfed. And they didn't.

Darlene and Marie continued to sew on Lottie's treadle Singer machine. As Marie advanced through 4-H and high school home economics classes Darlene, herself, learned the most advanced sewing techniques.

When Mrs. O"Leary from Paisley sponsored Marie in the "Make It Yourself with Wool " contest there was a trip over to Klamath Falls so that Lottie could buy 100% wool fabric at Miller's Department Store. A Butterick suit pattern was selected and Darlene and Marie put their heads together as they studied over each detail.

Marie's sewing projects had gone beyond Lottie's now obsolete methods and skills, however, she continued to provide the machine and the material. Bound button holes were required for the suit jacket and they were a challenge. One day Darlene had an idea, "Let's take the jacket down to Karilyn Story, she'll know what to do."

Karilyn and Dale Story were a young couple who worked for the Clark Ranch down at the south end of Abert Lake. Sometimes Karilyn and Dale came up to the ranch to play pinochle with Donald and

Darlene. In her unmarried days, which were not that long ago, Karilyn was a championship 4-H seamstress.

Down at the Clark ranch they lived in a little cabin behind the main house. Dale was an expert shot and he bragged about how he sat on the couch with a gun in his lap waiting for a skunk to poke its head through the hole around the pipes under the kitchen sink. As soon as he saw a head, he squeezed off a shot and they never once had a smell!

Donald tried that one time when they had some trouble with skunks getting into the attic, but he wasn't so lucky with the smell part.

One summer Lottie insisted that Donald order a fine grade of gravel to be spread in the drive between their two houses. When the contractors finished spreading the gravel there was a part of one load left over and they dumped the extra gravel in a pile under a spreading elm tree whose low branches provided perfect shade. It was between Lottie's front yard and the shop. Raymond and Sonny took their tonka trunks, tractors, plows and caterpillars and played there hour after hour.

In a perfect world such a life could go on forever, or so it seemed for those who had the privilege of living in God's country—at the ranch beneath Abert Rim. Lottie was a generous grandmother who lived on one side of the road where she let Marie keep her substantial wardrobe and all of her girly teenage trappings. There Marie had a nice bedroom with a set of twin beds and she easily entertained girlfriends overnight and on weekends.

Donald and Darlene lived in their rambling and occasionally expanding house across the creek, on the other side of the now graveled drive. One year Donald hired a professional carpenter who built a dining room addition onto the west side of their overburdened kitchen. Tables could be shoved together to stretch the length of both rooms when there were extra-large groups for Thanksgiving and branding.

Raymond and Sonny were growing up in the usual messy way of little boys. There were days when Marie's aggravation took over as she tried to press them into a state of refinement that met her teenage standards. It never worked. On the other hand, she loved them madly and dared anyone to say a bad thing about her little brothers. Overriding their boyish mess her heart was proud of them. Often, she envied Raymond's ramshackle way of attacking life while Sonny remained her pet.

During the spring of 1960 Marie finally completed a home economics project in which the students were required to make a child's garment. She decided to make a plaid flannel shirt for Sonny. It turned out to be a lot more complicated than what it first appeared and she never wanted to sew a piece of child's clothing again, but the end result turned out good. Mrs. Tainter held an afternoon tea for the various mothers where the children could model their clothing.

It was a lovely Lakeview kind of spring day at the very end of the school year. Old English Poplars and elms were full of their summer leaves and the grass of the school yard was a newly-mown velvet kind of green. Darlene walked from the car to the school in a proper fashion using the network of sidewalks, but Sonny could no longer contain himself. The minute he saw Marie coming to meet them he broke into a run and dashed straight across the lawn yelling out, "Where's my shirt, 'Ree, where's my shirt!"

# Endings and Beginnings

Marie went about ordinary tasks that she had come to take for granted during spring and summer. Some of those tasks she did for the very last time in her life. It was that pivotal spring and summer of 1961. She faced adulthood with a certain amount of dread mixed with anxious anticipation. Her body and parts of her awareness wanted to rush forward to experience the fulness of womanhood while the comforts of childhood, security of family and life at the ranch caused fear and doubt.

God, in His almighty wisdom, often casts a veil over our conscious day-to-day efforts so that we, mortal travelers on earth, will not recognize those last times for precisely what they are—last times. Life's funny that way.

Marie threw her saddle on Babe and made sure it was cinched up snug before she swung up and followed Dad and Raymond as they rode south toward the timber-culture to gather cattle for tomorrow's branding. It was a couple of years ago now when Dad had purchased both Babe and a new, but second-hand, saddle at an auction sale somewhere down south of Pine Creek. Lottie tried to not let on that she was more than half-way aggravated when Marie set up a saw horse smack dab in the middle of her front room where she proceeded to work the saddle into like-new condition with a generous amount of saddle soap.

Babe was a little mustang mare. She was a deep bay color with black mane, tail and stockings. Her mustang breeding showed through in her short stocky neck and rounded body. Donald said that she was a tough little horse and she turned out to be just that, plus she possessed a stout heart for traversing the rough terrain beneath Abert Rim.

When Marie wasn't there to ride Babe anymore and Donald's Cotteneye horse died an early death after gorging on green apples, Donald, himself, rode Babe for the rest of her cow-working days.

Out in the branding corral it was Marie's job to load the vaccine gun and keep a tally of steer calves and heifer calves. And then it was her duty to hustle to the house and clean up real quick-like so that she could help Mom get dinner on the table and help clean up the kitchen afterward. She honestly didn't mind that, or feel any particular resentment, because she liked cooking almost as much as she liked gathering cows and besides, there was always a crowd for branding and there was a holiday feeling about the entire day.

Although there was a lot of help out in the branding corral it was always Donald who applied the Lazy SC to the right flank of each calf. Marie understood, even back then, in 1961, that SC stood for Solomon Chandler, her and Raymond's and Sonny's great-grandfather. It was he who bought the ranch back in 1899. Lytle and Lottie had been able to register the Lazy SC when Lottie's father, Sol Chandler, had relinquished his brand.

Not long after graduation they trailed cattle across to Dicks Creek. It did cross Marie's mind that when they brought the cows home that fall, she'd be in Ashland at Southern Oregon College.

SOC, Southern Oregon College, (everyone called it SOC, pronounced just like sock) was the right place for Marie. It was a small college, not so overwhelming like the University of Oregon at Eugene, or Oregon State at Corvallis. She'd major in Journalism and if she didn't wind up getting married, or maybe even if she did get married, she'd become a writer for a magazine. She dreamed of writing for National Geographic. It *could* happen, she reckoned, but on the other hand it was a pretty outrageous idea for a country girl like her.

They sheared sheep the day after graduation. Marie got there for the tail-end of it. Nina Evans, one of her in-town friends, drove her out after the all-night graduation party up at the Elks' building.

High School graduation had turned out to be everything they said it would. There had been the prom and Mike Counts was her date for the prom. And then there were luncheons and teas galore and a new dress for each and every one of those occasions. She had a new pair of pointy toed high-heel shoes with miles and miles of narrow point. They were beautiful—a stylish marshmallow cream color. Most of the girls traded off those foot-destroying pointy-toed heels for a sensible pair of cute flats for the graduation party.

There was an extra amount of excitement about graduation that June of 1961 because Mark Hatfield, Governor of the State of Oregon, was scheduled to be the commencement speaker. He was a man of his word because when he had to turn down the class of 1960 he promised to speak for the class of '61, and he did.

Everyone in the near vicinity who received an announcement planned to attend and even some who did not receive an announcement. When the school board got wind about the size of the expected crowd, they decided to move the ceremony down to the larger auditorium/gymnasium/cafeteria of the Arthur D. Hay School.

Mark Hatfield was not only a man of his word; he was a class act. The graduating class was seated on the stage to the back of the speaker but Governor Hatfield turned around and spoke first to the class as he told them that although his back would be turned, his words were meant entirely for them. Marie never remembered the words he spoke, but she did always remember that he intended them for the graduating seniors—they were half thrilled with great anticipation and half scared to death.

Graduation was a hot sticky night.

Principal Delbert Mulholland gathered them outside the Arthur D. Hay gym on Saturday afternoon to practice for both Sunday night's Baccalaureate service and Monday night's graduation. He lined them up in their order of march and then he eyed the girls.

"Girls," Principal Mulholland said, "you cannot, I mean *cannot*, wear crinoline underskirts."

Many of the girls, including Marie, who loved that style beneath full skirts, let out a collective and audible gasp.

"Girls," he tried to carefully word his comments while the boys smothered their smirks, "you'll look ridiculous—like a bunch of circus clowns with your graduation gowns sticking out like a bunch of balloons."

The girls got his point and took his words seriously. In fact, that day of graduation practice was the last time Marie ever wore a crinoline slip.

Darlene helped Marie dress for graduation. Although Darlene didn't say so, something about her loving admiration conveyed a message to her daughter. Darlene tied the narrow ice-blue velveteen sash into a perfect bow at the front waist. Marie had made the dress herself. It was white lawn with thin stripes of tiny blue blossoms. A simple bodice with round neck and short sleeves with a gathered skirt was set off by that narrow blue velveteen slash.

Darlene ran her hands over the skirt as it swirled around Marie's slender legs. The girl who had once considered herself big, awkward and out of place as a grade-school child had ceased to grow somewhere in time and now she was one of the smaller girls in her class. Her brown hair that she once considered drab glinted almost a deep auburn in the sunshine. Early that morning she had washed it and done it up on brush rollers. When she took it down in the late afternoon, she expertly brushed it out and teased it into a stylish, but demure amount of pouf.

As Darlene smoothed Marie's skirt, she was secretly glad for the principal's ban on those outrageous stiff, nylon netting slips, "Your dress is perfect. It looks so drapey and so much cooler. It's such a hot night."

"Drapey," Marie thought, "how perfect. Like something out of a fashion magazine."

She loved her mother for saying absolute perfect words. Perfect words that gave her a smidgeon of grown-up confidence.

That summer Darlene and Marie spent hours sewing together. Lottie bought most of the material and patterns, whatever Marie and Darlene decided on and together they planned her college wardrobe. There were trips to Klamath and one trip to Boise, Idaho to buy whatever they needed. When the shopping was complete Marie had just the right amount of Pendleton skirts and Jantzen sweaters plus an outrageous over-the-top pair of navy-blue flats. The upper part of those shoes was made of stiffened velvet. They were *so* in style and *so* perfect and *so* impractical.

All of the Lakeview girls enrolled at SOC signed up for dorm rooms in Suzanne Hall. There was a brand-new girl's dormitory called Cascade Hall, but Lakeview girls stayed in Suzanne Hall. Using new-found college slang, they called it Suzy Hall. One of Marie's friends, Claudia Harris, asked Marie to be her roommate, but Marie was determined to take on adulthood with its full measure. Marie thanked Claudia but said she was going to take her chances on a roommate so that she could widen her scope of friendships. Claudia said that she understood and she just wished that she had that much courage.

Courage. A mighty big word for a little country girl from Valley Falls.

Freshman week at Southern Oregon College arrived. Everything was neatly packed into the back of Grandmo's good car. Grandmo's good car had become a green Rambler Ambassador Station Wagon.

Everyone was excited and everyone was going along: Dad, Mom, Grandmo, Raymond and Sonny. It had been an odd feeling when Raymond and Sonny left for the school bus on Tuesday after Labor Day while Marie stayed home. She felt a certain amount of grownup freedom, but at the same time there was a nagging pit in her stomach at the loss of old familiar days.

That year was Sonny's first day of first grade.

Donald pulled up in front of Suzanne Hall and Marie hurried in to register and get her room assignment. The upper-classman at the desk checked over her list. "Marie Simms. I can't find you on the list. Oh yes, there's been a change and you have been assigned over in Cascade Hall. Aren't you excited? It's just beautiful. Everything is so new and modern."

Courage! Where was that courage now?

Claudia breezed by with a suitcase in each hand. "Oh Marie, isn't it wonderful? I hear you're going to be in Cascade and so is Ruthie Troxell. You and Ruthie are only two from Lakeview who were lucky enough to get rooms over there.

Marie was willing to make a new friend in a new roommate, but she wanted to be on the same floor in the same dorm with the rest of her Lakeview friends.

Cascade Hall was nice and it was modern as modern can be. The rooms had tall windows that let in tons of natural light; twin beds were smartly shoved beneath built-in storage units creating couch-like day-beds and all the girls were friendly as they traipsed up and down the hallways. College girls ran up and down stairs directing overladen dads whose arms were filled with baggage and boxes. The male gender was allowed on upper floors of the dorm for that one day only, so that fathers and brothers could lend muscle for the move-in.

Marie's roommate was a girl from Coos Bay whose last name also began with the letter "S." Ruthie Troxell was settling-in down the hall with a girl whose last name began with "T." Marie's roommate did not want to be at SOC, she would rather be at Oregon State and she never let anyone forget that. By spring term, she finally got her wish.

It was all good. Marie laughed and studied with a wonderful group of new friends. The Dorm Mother was a kindly grandmother to all of her charges. Marie turned out to be somewhat unique according to the other girls because she lived on a big ranch in Eastern Oregon.

She was extremely popular on Sunday evenings of those weekends when she happened to snag a ride home. Darlene picked up her cue of what was required of her in her new role as the mother of a college girl. She sent Marie back to SOC with a newspaper lined paste-board box filled with homemade roast beef or ham sandwiches, cookies and fruit enough for a gaggle of hungry girls waiting for a taste of home-made food.

When Dad drove away and left her standing on the steps of Cascade Hall that Sunday morning of mid-September in 1961, she didn't cry. She wanted to, but she didn't. She watched until she saw Grandmo's green Ambassador disappear into the traffic of Siskiyou Boulevard then she turned and went up the stairs to her new room on the freshman floor of Cascade Hall.

She pretended not to think about home as she continued to unpack and settle her room. Andrea, her roommate, chattered away. Andrea was pretending not to think about how she would rather be at Oregon State. They pretended a lot during those first two terms of college while Andrea suffered through SOC. By the time Andrea left, Marie was well-settled into life at Cascade Hall.

Marie settled into a new kind of contentment. She knew that to the east, over the southern end of the Cascade Mountains, was the Klamath Basin. Farther east, over Bly Mountain and Quartz Mountain, was Goose Lake Valley and Lakeview. To the north of Goose Lake Valley, the landscape drops into Crooked Creek Valley. And on northward, through the canyon where Crooked Creek only manages a slight trickle of water during late summer and early fall, the land curls out to the edge of the high-desert and the wide-open country of Valley Falls.

Abert Rim stands guard over the eastern edge of the valley and there—right there—snugged up against the rim's foothills is the ranch.

It turned out that if she could manage to remember the geographic location of Abert Rim, then she knew where she was. She knew where Abert Rim is when she lived on the gulf coast of eastern Texas. She knew when she lived beside the Columbia River up in The Dalles and later on she knew when she lived farther west on the Columbia River, in Portland, where her son was born.

She can look out her windows now and see Black Cap as it watches over Lakeview. Raymond also lives in Lakeview these days. He has a cabin up on the old summer range of the ranch. It overlooks that little meadow where Dicks Creek pushes through tall June grass.

Twenty-three miles, give or take a mile or two up Highway 395, Marie often drives her red Subaru north from Lakeview to Valley Falls. A graveled road turns due east toward the rim. She travels over the dusty county road as it swings back to the south, and at the very end of the road is the SC Ranch. That's what Sonny and his son call the ranch nowadays, here in the twenty-first century.

Made in the USA
Columbia, SC
18 July 2021